Donald Brittain
Never The Ordinary Way

FROM THE NATIONAL FILM BOARD OF CANADA

Donald Brittain
Never The Ordinary Way

FROM THE NATIONAL FILM BOARD OF CANADA

Copyright © 1991 The National Film Board of Canada
All rights reserved. No part of this publication may be reproduced or used
in any form or by any means without written permission of the publisher.

Edited by Terry Kolomeychuk with the assistance of T.L. Coles and Duncan Thornton

Graphic Design: Margaret Kampff / Doowah Design Inc.
Text set in Goudy 11 pt./16 pt

Canadian Cataloguing in Publication Data
Eulogy by William Weintraub, essays by Ronald Blumer and Rick Groen
Includes a filmography and bibliographic references
DSS cat. no. NF2–51/1991E
1. Brittain, Donald
2. Motion-picture producers and directors – Canada – Biography
3. Documentary films – Canada – Production and direction
I. Kolomeychuk, Terry.   II. National Film Board of Canada.   III. Title: Donald Brittain: Never the ordinary way.
PN1998.3.B74D66 1991 070.1'8'092 C90–098687–5
ISBN 0–7722–0188–9

First published in 1991 in Winnipeg by National Film Board of Canada,
245 Main Street, Winnipeg, Manitoba, R3C 1A7
Distributed in Canada by the National Film Board of Canada, Winnipeg,
Montreal, Halifax, Ottawa, Toronto, Saskatoon, Edmonton, Vancouver
Manufactured in Canada.
First Printing, 1991.
1 2 3 4 5 6 7 8 9 10 / 95 94 93 92 91

The Editors would like to acknowledge the
contributions of the following to this publication:
Brigitta Brittain
Marrin Canell
Ray Harper, Access Network
John Spotton, NFB
Caroline Forcier, Moving Image & Sound Archives
Adam Symansky, NFB
Doug Kiefer, CSC
Steven Rosenberg, Doowah Design Inc.
Karyn Fedun, M & KF Advertising
Madeleine Proulx, Rideau Hall
Heather Graham, Academy of Canadian Cinema and Television
Roman Kroitor, IMAX Systems
Cathy Markou, CBC Business Affairs
Karen Marginson, NFB
Bernard Lutz, NFB
Rose-Aimee Todd, NFB

NFB and all NFB productions mentioned in this publication are trademarks of the National Film Board of Canada.

CBC and all CBC productions mentioned in this publication are trademarks of the Canadian Broadcasting Corporation.

A Day With Donald Brittain by Rick Groen.
Copyright © 1989 by Rick Groen. Reprinted by permission of The Globe and Mail.

A Eulogy For Donald Brittain by William Weintraub.
Copyright © 1989 by William Weintraub. Reprinted by permission of the author.

Table of Contents

The Man

A Eulogy For Donald Brittain

by William Weintraub

As read at the funeral service
Christ Church Cathedral, Montreal
July 26, 1989

How fortunate we are to have known Donald Brittain. How unfortunate we are not to have him with us a while longer. But if his life was too short, it was still a life fulfilled, a life abundant. And it was long enough for him to create a legacy that is beyond compare.

MEMORANDUM…BETHUNE…VOLCANO…THE CHAMPIONS… The list is astonishingly long. And in his house, up on Clarke Avenue, the shelf groans under the weight of the Etrogs, the Genies, the Emmys, the Nellies—a little forest of statuettes with odd names. And on the walls, more awards and certificates and parchments from Edinburgh, Venice, Sydney, Leipzig, New York, Sofia, San Francisco.

This recognition was for films that resound with intimations of immortality. People will want to see them decades from now, even centuries from now. They will be remembered.

But today, on this occasion, I think our memories are more of the man than of his work. And what an extraordinary man was Donald Brittain! Wise, compassionate, complicated, exasperating, funny, melancholy, irritating, contrary, surprising, endlessly entertaining, brilliant, generous—and beloved by such a legion of friends and colleagues.

2

But above all—extraordinary. Donald seemed incapable of doing anything in an ordinary way. He was not striving for effect, it was just that he had never mastered the ordinary way. For him, the shortest distance between two points could never be a straight line, a boring line.

His clothes, for instance. Can't you see him now, shuffling down those forbidding corridors of the film Board in that resplendent brown baseball jacket? The corrugated trousers are clinging desperately to the hipbones. People are following him. Are they anxious to see if the uncertain suspension of the trousers will finally collapse? No, they are following him because they want to talk to him. Everybody wanted to talk to Don.

His clothes. Do you remember those strange, shirt-like garments he used to wear in the seventies? What would you call them? Abbreviated caftans? Mu-mus? He had them made for him by some little old dressmaker. They weren't exactly fashion, but by George they had style. Donald always had style, in everything he did.

That fact started dawning on us one day in 1963, in Theatre Six, when we watched the cutting copy of a film called FIELDS OF SACRIFICE. Donald had arrived at the Film Board, at the old sawmill on John Street, in Ottawa, nine years earlier. He was an unemployed journalist who thought he might try his hand at writing for films.

In the years that followed, he learned his craft and paid his dues, making all those solemnly useful films like SURVIVAL IN THE ARCTIC and SETTING FIRES FOR SCIENCE. Now they'd sent him to Europe to make a film about the graves of Canadian soldiers who

Donald always had style…

3

had died in two wars. It was another useful film, another film that nobody else wanted to make. But Donald astonished us. He came back with a masterpiece. His first masterpiece.

Up till then, old Don had been just one of the boys—working hard, making good films and telling lies in the tavern. But now we began to suspect that we had a poet in our midst. But of course we were too polite to tell him that.

How the man could write! Is there any one of us who can't hear that voice right now?... The cadence, the drone, the rasp, the music, the words. The words. What writer has not envied the way he could find that word, that precisely right word, the word that would stab, that would chill, that would glow in the dark. He would sit at that ramshackle typewriter at three o'clock in the morning, enveloped in a miasma of cigarette smoke, waiting for the word. And it would come to him.... What a gift! What talent! What discipline!

As we all know, the words were so very important to his films. It was the words that led an American critic to write that "Donald Brittain purges the documentary of its usual sluggishness and timidity."

Don refused to let anything he was ever involved in be boring. And nowhere was this more evident than at the poker table. The most dramatic hands were surely those where old Don had a lot at stake. He could take an astonishingly long time making up his mind whether he should bet or fold. And he would mutter away at length, making us privy to the convoluted thought processes that he

...old Don had been just one of the boys —

was bringing to bear on his dilemma. It could be highly irritating. But how we're going to miss that divine irritation! How diminished that poker table is going to be, from now on—if we ever have the heart to resume it.

Don was fascinated by time. Getting into his car one day, he clicked on his stopwatch. Why? He was driving to the Film Board via the Côte des Neiges route and he had to know exactly how long it would take. Yesterday he had taken the Victoria Avenue route and he had timed that. In fact he had been timing the two routes all week.

But mind you, we still arrived at the Film Board an hour late for his appointment. Why? We had been detained on Clarke Avenue for the completion of a task. Donald had produced a list of all the production people at the Film Board and we had to assign a military rank to each person. Which cameraman was a captain, which gaffer was a sergeant, which administrator was a major, who were the colonels and who were the brigadiers. It was important for Donald to have things like that worked out with precision.

Life was an endless game for Donald, but he was not a frivolous man. His films were laced with humor and irony, but they were very serious films. They were concerned with the fate of the planet, with the abuse of power, with the folly and corruption of politics, with genocide, with the abuse of the weak by the strong.

And his films were concerned with Canada, the country he loved so much, the country that exasperated him so much, the country he always came back to. As much as any man, Donald Brittain held up a mirror, so his country could see itself—its truth, its beauty, its sordidness, its glory.

Donald wrote a little—not enough—about how he made his films. "A documentary crew," he once wrote, "is like a small band of adventurers, thrown together in desperate enterprise, totally reliant on each other for survival, charged with the job of bringing something back alive, and thus hopefully illuminate some corner of the human spirit."

A colleague of his put it somewhat differently: "It was like going out on a trapeze, without a net. You had to remember that he never dropped you before."

Don always chose the path of risk. It was part of his inability to settle for the obvious. His working methods were also those of greatest risk. Deadlines loomed, and little seemed to be getting done. Fear would start to invade the cutting room. But Don would reassure his colleagues. "I function best," he once said, "in an advanced state of panic."

Brutally long hours, weekends, vacations postponed—but his colleagues loved it, and they came back for more. Because if Donald worked them like slaves, he himself was the hardest-working of them all.

"A documentary crew is like a small band of adventurers..."

He respected his crews, he genuinely wanted their suggestions and criticisms, he gave them generous credit for everything they did. Everybody wanted to work with Don Brittain. There was so much he could teach you. And, above all, it was such great, agonizing fun. What loyalty he inspired! And what loyalty he gave back in return!

Don Brittain's talent came to fruition in that dumb and dreary decade called the sixties, when so many of our young filmmakers were idealogues, always ready to jump onto the next trendy bandwagon. The bandwagon is always the refuge of the untalented. But Donald was different. His films were about people, not slogans. As one critic said, "He makes the common person great, the famous person common."

He made films about many famous people, and I wonder what kind of a film he would have made about Donald Code Brittain. There would probably have been too much horse-racing in it for my own taste. There might even have been some documentary ambiguity in it, to make it appear that the expensive horse Don once bought had won more than that one solitary race.

The Ottawa Rough Riders would have been it in, with their greatest fan, Don Brittain, cheering them on, perhaps because they were the losingest team in human history. And there would have been the young Don making a brilliant play in the touch football game behind the Film Board. And Don as the captain of a basketball team called The Prockets, playing illegally on the NFB soundstage.

There would have been lots of golf in this award-winning epic. A young actor, fresh-faced and bright-eyed, would have the role of teen-age Don, playing with his father at the Royal Ottawa Golf Club. And there would be yesterday's Don, played by himself, playing on the Dunany course, up in Lachute, with his son, Christopher. And here we

would see documentary truth, with Christopher patiently showing his father how to do it. "Just relax, Dad, and swing easy." And Don would show himself in close-up, smiling and proud that he could learn from his son. And proud that he could learn from his beloved daughter, Jennifer, who knows a lot about horses, and about Canada.

And there would be his wife, Brigitta, pillar of strength, shelter in the storm, rescuer from the chaos that he loved to create—beloved centre of his life.

Brigitta, Christopher, Jennifer—there would be a lot of good stuff about them, in that film. And there would be cleverly cut, cameo appearances by a lot of his friends. He'd be down there in the Film Board basement, in the pit, at four in the morning, hunched over the Steenbeck, enveloped in a cloud of smoke, trying to crowd as many as possible into that film that he ought to have made.

For the narration he might well have again used those lines of Norman Bethune's:

An artist enters eagerly into the life of man, of all men.
He becomes all men in himself.
The function of the artist is to disturb.
His duty is to arouse the sleeper, to shake the complacent
*   pillars of the world.*
He reminds the world of its dark ancestry, shows the world its
*   present, and points the way to its new birth.*
He makes uneasy the static, the set and the still.

...Donald Brittain held up a mirror, so his country could see itself...

8

A Day With Donald Brittain

by Rick Groen
Globe and Mail, July 24, 1989

That day, three precious summers ago, Donald Brittain stood happy in the winner's circle. For a while, things had been tough. His landmark, internationally acclaimed documentaries— MEMORANDUM, HENRY FORD'S AMERICA, NEVER A BACKWARD STEP, PAPERLAND, the searing VOLCANO: AN INQUIRY INTO THE LIFE AND DEATH OF MALCOLM LOWRY—all seemed long behind him. "I was as down as a snake's belly." he would say of that time. "For once, my confidence was shook. But then the Hal Banks thing came along." The Banks thing—his much-lauded CANADA'S SWEETHEART—proved sweet indeed, an aesthetic triumph that banished the hyphen from the "docu-drama," perhaps the film world's first certifiable cold-fusion of those warring elements. His career revived, he was already working on the next project, an ambitious chronicle of Mackenzie King, working as he always did— fitfully at the outset, in a white heat as the deadline loomed. Yes, Brittain was riding high again.

That day began early, with a morning session in the studio of a young director. He was leasing his voice—that instantly identifiable rasp—to her narrative soundtrack. Everyone wanted a piece of that voice, but Brittain used it best in his own films reading his own words. Writing was his first love, and he nurtured it carefully, respectfully. His scripts were a model of economy and precision.

Session over, he paused to commune with his favored travelling companions—the cigarette, the bottle—and then headed off for a radio interview on CBC's Morningside. Brittain freely acknowledged the debt he owed to the twin public institutions, the National Film Board and CBC television, that showcased his basically non-commercial talent. But his real allegiance was to words, to still images, and to radio. "I really feel that in a sense everything went backwards," he once mused. "If I had my druthers, you'd start with super wide-screen motion pictures and then you'd freeze the frame and have radio and stills."

In fact, CBC-style radio and Brittain-made film have a lot in common: both somehow convey the essence of a hard-to-define country; both are passionate yet detached, intimate yet ironic; and both are generously praised but largely under-valued. So the interview went well and, brushing yet another ash from his perma-rumpled pants, the subject headed out.

Everyone wanted a piece of that voice...

That day, that's when the fun began. Brittain had just bought a racehorse. Not a very good one, a filly who shared a trait with her new owner—each had a life-long habit of following the horses. For Brittain loved the sport in the way he loved so many other things—unsentimentally, even sardonically. The way he loved baseball and history, for example. In the dishevelled study of his Montreal home, a cap from the long-defunct St. Louis Browns sat rakishly atop a clay bust of the long-dead Edward VII—the need to revere competing with the urge to debunk.

His horse was scheduled to run on the afternoon card, and Brittain spent several hours in the paddock with the trainers, the exercise boys, the sewers of silks—the track's Runyanesque litany. He listened far more than he talked. That was the observer in him, the measured documentarian. And he delighted in the whole scene: the sport of kings, the obsession of commoners, it was the perfect paradox for a man who could describe himself as "a socialist, a royalist, and an Ottawa Roughriders fan."

He also revelled in racing parlance, especially in the track-siders' habit of speaking in a perpetual present tense. "My horse wins yesterday," a trainer would say. Of course, that's precisely how Brittain approached the past in his own work, how he dissected history and the men who made it—the Kings, the Fords, the Trudeaus, the Lévesques—carving away at the detritus to find its current drama, its universal nub, its power to illuminate the here and now. Trudeau wins yesterday.

His horse started badly that day, trailing again. And then it happened. Maybe she smelled the glue that would have followed the next defeat. Or maybe it was just that day. But she surged, passing

one horse, another and another, finally winning, as the parlance has it, "going away." Brittain, standing off by himself in the grandstand, beamed. And then something else happened. The bags seemed to lighten beneath his eyes, the stoop to vanish from his gait, and he bounded down to the track like a skittish colt. There, still beaming, he stood happy in the winner's circle, a boy again in the afternoon sun.

The artist wins, going away, because his art remains. But sometimes, so do the sensibilities of the man who forged it, living on to brighten a little the here and now. And so it must be said: Last Friday, three precious summers later, Donald Brittain dies. Present tense; present with us.

"…a socialist, a royalist, and an Ottawa Roughriders fan."

The Filmmaker

The Filmmaker

by Ron Blumer

"Sure he liked fame, but that isn't why he did what he did. He was truly driven to make great films—the only way he could be happy was to make the best films he could make. There was no alternative possible."

Adam Symansky, producer

"He held a mirror up to us—he could have done it nicely and safely but he always took the way of greatest risk. It is going to be a lonely country without Donald Brittain."

Sean McCann, actor

"We are the only nation whose national symbol is a policeman. I fear that Canadians have an obsession with security. Our artists' imaginations are dulled, exploring the unknown is too much work, and we settle into the gentle pursuit of mediocrity. I'm told we are the most heavily insured people on earth. We should never forget that when all things are secure, no man is safe."
Donald Brittain

Producer Adam Symansky worked closely with Donald Brittain during the last five years of his life. "In trying to understand Brittain, you are trying to understand how a poet works," Symansky says. "He was someone who, with a few brush strokes, was able to capture some essence of the human condition. You see the finished films and it looks so simple, but I saw the struggle; I know how hard he worked. I'd leave the cutting room at three in the morning and I'd come back the next day and he'd still be hunched over the typewriter surrounded by a pile of crumpled-up paper. He would have written only two lines and he would rewrite those two lines several times and rework them even as he was recording the final narration."

Brittain wasn't always so hard-working. Indeed, in his early days at the Film Board, he barely managed to hold onto his job. Brittain came to the NFB in 1954 after a brief career as a newspaper reporter, and he did not adapt easily to his new profession. "I spent a few years writing scripts which everyone seemed to hate," he later recalled. "No films ever got made. I kept hearing that they were going

to fire me, so I kept a low profile. There was this place where you were sent before they fired you, corridor 'W' in back of the third floor. The smell of death hung over me when I was informed that my office was being moved there. Seventy-five bucks a week, and I knew my days were numbered."

In fact, Brittain's filmmaking career was just beginning. He was working in the NFB's sponsor unit, which made utilitarian films commissioned by government departments and the occasional corporation. The Film Board trained novices at the sponsor unit, and, according to Brittain, the films he made there were pretty bad. "Church basement stuff, but the sponsor liked them, so I was saved." Brittain's first real break came in 1960, when he was given the job of figuring out what to do with several million feet of World War II footage sitting in the Film Board vaults. He turned it into CANADA AT WAR (1962), an impressive 13-part television series. This led to an assignment to produce a film on the most unpromising of subjects—Canadian war graves abroad. It was a project which nobody at the Film Board had wanted to touch, but Brittain transformed it into a film that everyone wished they had made. In FIELDS OF SACRIFICE (1963), with its brilliant editing and tough, yet compassionate narration, Brittain had at last discovered his voice.

Film Board producer Bill Weintraub paid tribute to that voice after Brittain's death: "How the man could write!…The cadence, the drone, the rasp, the music, the words…the way he could find that word, that precisely right word, the word that would stab, that would chill, that would glow in the dark."

"Making a documentary is like big game hunting..."

Brittain followed FIELDS OF SACRIFICE with his first wave of brilliant films, beginning with BETHUNE (1964) and including such early classics as MEMORANDUM (1964) and NEVER A BACKWARD STEP (1965). During the mid-1970s Brittain began a second wave of masterpieces that left the critics breathless. Beginning with VOLCANO (1976), a film about the author Malcolm Lowry, and culminating in PAPERLAND (1979), his irreverent look at life among the bureaucrats, he astounded audiences. His subjects ranged from baseball to Henry Ford II. He made 'people' films and 'idea' films, 'pretty picture' films and 'interview' films. But they all had his particular stamp, a quality which film critic Rick Groen has described as "a communion of words and pictures that is simultaneously detached yet passionate, ironic yet involved." Describing Brittain's style seems to require this sort of paradox; those who attempt to pin down the nature of his unique talent usually become tongue-tied in a mass of conflicting adjectives.

For Brittain himself, the challenge was simply "to make documentary as entertaining as Cary Grant." "I have a strong desire to make documentaries as entertainment," he explained. "To do this, I always try to stay one step ahead of the audience—to surprise them and to lead them in a direction which is unexpected." No matter how exalted the subject matter, Brittain always pitched his films to the guys in the back of the tavern. His aim was "to move them emotionally, reach them in the gut."

As Adam Symansky observes, "He was really good at figuring out what people would want to know. What did they really want to know about Mackenzie King or Hal Banks or Bethune? Not the philosophical or political issues, but what they ate for breakfast and

what they discussed with their wives—what kind of gum they chewed. Don read the comics, he loved sports; he never felt above his audience. Just because he was making 'art' didn't mean that he forgot the People Magazine, the gossip part of the story." The question for Brittain was always how you transform the gossip into something that illustrates the soul of a person.

Brittain's strongest works—and indeed the vast majority of his films—were biographical. Using both documentary and dramatic techniques, he painted moving portraits of such diverse subjects as Lord Thomson of Fleet, Tommy Douglas, René Lévesque, Pierre Trudeau, Hal Banks, and Malcolm Lowry.

Brittain's career blossomed at the time of a great revolution in the development of documentary film. Until the 1960s, documentaries had been cumbersome to shoot. The huge cameras, lights and sound trucks needed had meant that documentaries had to be pre-scripted like feature films, but in the sixties, hand-held cameras and portable sound recording equipment suddenly made it possible to go out and catch bits of reality on the run. The problem was what to do with the hundreds of thousands of feet of 'reality' once you got it back to the cutting room.

With a sixth sense for structure, and the "golden hinge" of his narration, Brittain had the answers. He realized that unleashing the power of this new medium required a whole new attitude towards the filmmaking process—a flexibility that was the exact reverse of the old, pre-scripted approach. "Making a documentary is like big-game hunting," he said. "You go out with a great cameraman and soundman to capture something and bring it back. You don't control it—you surround it. A lot of guys go rigid; they say, 'I'm the director,

I'm in charge and I'm going to overpower the material.' That's a terrible mistake. When you are out there shooting, you are collecting raw material and that's all."

He described the documentary crew as "a small band of adventurers thrown together in a desperate enterprise, totally reliant on each other for survival and charged with the job of bringing something back alive. Filmmaking, unlike writing and other solitary forms, is a gregarious pursuit; the heat of the moment welds men and women together into a creative unit. When it's over, you don't forget each other. At night you spin tales of old campaigns. It is something that grown-ups have difficulty understanding."

Brittain's co-workers felt this bond very strongly. Ted Remerowski, who worked with Brittain as an editor, describes how "he made you feel like a co-conspirator." Doug Keifer, one of Brittain's favorite cameramen, recalls that Brittain "always made you part of the filmmaking process. Donald was the orchestra conductor—he was unquestionably the leader and set the direction of the filming—but he was confident enough to turn to you during a shoot and say, 'I just don't know what to do next.' I probably did the best work of my life with him."

Once the shooting was completed, a Donald Brittain film was forged during long days and tortured nights in the editing room. "Being in a cutting room with Don was like being on a voyage of discovery," according to Marrin Canell, a producer who worked extensively with Brittain. "He never had preconceived notions of how the film should be structured—that's what always amazed me. The final form never came easily, it was always a struggle."

"He made you feel like a co-conspirator..."

In an interview with *Cinema Canada*, Brittain described the difficult process of editing the Holocaust documentary MEMORANDUM (1965). "I don't know how many times we put that thing together. At one stage it was too predictable, at another it was too confusing. Certain things which laid an egg at the beginning of the film became wonderful at the end. We had cut ninety-two sequences which were never used in the final film. Nine months in the editing room and I never thought the thing would work." According to Canell, Brittain's struggle was largely "because he never went for the obvious. Most filmmakers put together a film using a paste-up of the transcripts. He always listened and watched the footage to see not only what the subjects said, but how they said it. He let the material work on him, choosing the shots on the basis of his emotional reaction—always looking for the little moments that exposed the characters and their idiosyncracies."

Despite the long and numbing editing process, Brittain had an uncanny ability to remain fresh to new ideas. He would project the various rough versions to invited audiences and closely watch their reactions to see what was working and what was not. He would fight for endless hours trying to make a shot or a sequence work, but if it did not, he would throw it away without regret. When Les Rose was a young filmmaker in the basement of the Film Board, he watched Brittain's activity in the neighbouring cutting room with awe. "I'd edit a sequence and it would be fat—too much material. Brittain chops to the bone. When he gets finished with a sequence, there is practically blood dripping off the editing machine."

Brittain, like Mozart, never sought to do things differently than his predecessors, only better.

20

And always the 'bone' for Brittain was the story—the glimpse into the soul, the insight into what made the human animal tick. Like a novelist, he was always after the incident, the look or the gesture—the key that revealed inner character.

Robert Duncan worked as a researcher and writer on some of Brittain's biographical films. He recalls, "We consumed our subjects and they consumed us. Through Brittain I learned that it was not enough just to say that a person was born and he went to school. You had to explain that it had been a long labour and a difficult birth and tell how he was feeling on that first day of school. It was the little golden nuggets of information that Brittain loved and made us love."

Brittain's first biographical film was about the Canadian doctor and crusader Norman Bethune. "I was so totally involved that I thought I knew the guy personally," Brittain said in a magazine interview. "For a whole year I sweated blood to put it together. I started out as a Bethune hero-worshipper and gradually got to the point where I really disliked the man intensely. Finally came the long process of trying to round him out. I remember the day it was finished. I walked home and stayed under the covers for twenty-four hours; my nerves were shot. Then we screened the film for Bethune's friends, many of whom were alive and kicking—some of whom had slept with him. That was the great moment for me: they liked the film."

In 1968, at the height of his career, Don Brittain quit his secure National Film Board staff job for the precarious life of a freelancer. "I am essentially a very lazy person," he later explained. "I got into a situation at the Film Board where I could spend all my

21

time at committee meetings, and it's easier to sit on a committee than to make a film. It is very different as a hired gun—greed is a great spur to my creativity." In the next ten years, Brittain built a freelance career. Most of his films were still made for the Film Board, but many were also joint projects with the CBC. It was a unique position, and it enabled Brittain to draw on the strengths of both organizations—the creative freedom of the Film Board and the huge audience of the television network.

In the mid-seventies Brittain also tried working for Hollywood, but he quickly came to hate the place. "I don't think the man was capable of compromise." explains actor Sean McCann, "He could compromise with time, he could compromise with budget, but he couldn't compromise with content." But compromise was essential to working in Hollywood, and as Brittain said later, the experience taught him how much freedom he needed: "Essentially, I'm not interested in big budgets unless I've got some control. The more money I have, the less elbow room I've got. In big-budget films the money men come in to watch the dailies and start objecting to somebody blinking an eye in shot 27b, take 4. Hell, I'd rather go back to the newspaper business."

Within the year, Brittain gave up on Hollywood and began again to make a stream of award-winning Canadian films. With his

"He would talk more than the actor."

22

own projects and those he produced for others, he often worked on several films a year. But Brittain had always feared becoming stale, and the more films he made, the stronger that fear became. By the early 1980s, despite continuing success, he confessed to a close friend that he felt his creative life had come to an end. "I've had a good kick at the can," he said, "maybe it's time I threw in the towel." But instead of quitting, Brittain changed direction and gave himself a new set of challenges making dramatic films. He had attempted drama now and then throughout his career, directing scripts written by other people, but he had never really felt in control. Not surprisingly then, his first real success in drama was with a film he both wrote and directed, CANADA'S SWEETHEART: THE SAGA OF HAL C. BANKS (1985), the story of the union-busting thug Hal Banks. In CANADA'S SWEETHEART, critic Rick Groen wrote, Brittain finally "banished the hyphen from the 'docu-drama', perhaps the world's first certifiable cold fusion of those warring elements." The form of the film was a unique Brittain creation—a narrated drama. His working methods were equally unconventional.

"The casting sessions were very bizarre," according to the film's producer, Adam Symansky. "He would talk more than the actor. You would sit there while Don, in excruciating detail, would tell the actor the whole sub-text and who this person was and so on. Some of them really got into it, but most of them just wanted some lines to read. He would finally hand the guy a page with a few dozen words. There was never any attempt to make him act. That was forbidden. It was not the orthodox way, but somehow he came out of it with a feeling of whether this guy would work or not."

"All of the stylistic details which normally obsess dramatic directors bored him to tears. He never used to bother himself with details of set design or costume or camera angles. What he did care about was getting a good performance out of the actors. While filming, he never watched the cameraman, he watched the actors—watched and listened intently to each word and its inflection. That's where he gave his strongest direction. And if they felt they hadn't got it right, he would always give them another chance to do it better."

Actor Sean McCann worked in CANADA'S SWEETHEART and THE KING CHRONICLE. He remembers Brittain as the director who "would never let you get set in your ways. He would always be pushing you off guard, doing things like handing you a speech five minutes before filming. I couldn't possibly prepare and as a consequence I would be reaching—stretching. I would be uncomfortable but after the film was finished, I couldn't wait to work with him again."

Brittain's working methods meant that chaos always seemed to engulf his dramatic productions. For starters, there never seemed to be a final shooting script. During filming, with crew, lights, actors and extras waiting, you would see Brittain off in a corner of the set, furiously writing the next page of dialogue.

"Brittain would never let you get set in your ways."

"He would always want to let ideas ferment as long as he possibly could," according to Symansky. "He needed all the sub-text to work with—the feeling of the society, of the times, what other people felt—as much surrounding material as possible: the books people were reading at that time or the fact the Red Sox had lost the Pennant. He loved the context in which things happened and he would build out of that context the truth of a particular moment or a particular person. His technique was to immerse himself in the material so that it would always be running through his head. That's why he waited until the last minute to write things down."

When the shooting was finished, Brittain approached his dramatic material in much the same way that he did his documentaries. He treated the footage he had shot simply as raw material—blocks to be moved, and re-moved, during a long and arduous editing process. Editing completed, he would narrate the drama, using his unseen voice to provide the emphasis and the links to unite often disparate scenes. The net result was neither drama nor documentary, but a hybrid which combined the emotional involvement of fiction with the realism and immediacy of a documentary. It was a new art form which belonged only to him.

For his associates, making films with Donald Brittain was both nerve-wracking and exhilarating. Adam Symansky once compared the

With a sixth sense for structure...
Brittain had all the answers.

25

process to "going out with him on a trapeze without a net. You just had to keep reminding yourself that he had never dropped you before." Nothing ever seemed to gel until the film was finished, and it was never finished until the last possible second. For Brittain, the creative process was long and messy, but the films were the pay-off; each one a breakthrough, a sign that he had pushed back his boundaries a little more. It was a 35-year, 100-film battle, and he never did get stale. Perhaps he stayed fresh because he always took the most risky path, says producer Bill Weintraub—"It was part of his inability to settle for the obvious. He seemed incapable of doing anything in an ordinary way."

Brittain believed film was a great medium for storytelling, and he was the greatest of storytellers. On location, he was a superb interviewer, and in the editing room, a magician with structure. His dramas are bold experiments on uncharted seas; his documentaries, models of cinematic art. In the end, however, we will continue to watch his films because they offer us insights into ourselves, into other people and into the human condition. Detached yet passionate, ironic yet involved, throughout his long and varied career Brittain found endless fascination in the foibles of the human animal. Perhaps the quote from Sophocles which Brittain used to begin VOLCANO sums up his own philosophy: "Wonders are many, and none is more wonderful than man."

The Films

Fields of Sacrifice

1963
38 Minutes

FIELDS OF SACRIFICE was Brittain's first masterpiece. Unlike his later films, which mix stock footage, cinema verite sequences and interviews, this early film succeeds using only images and Brittain's powerful narration.

Commissioned by the Department of Veterans Affairs, FIELDS OF SACRIFICE was to have been typical of the sponsored films that were the bread and butter of the Film Board. The Department had wanted a travelogue of the war graves of Canadians who died abroad in the service of their country, a film to show Canadians that the graves were being well tended. Brittain took this most unpromising of subjects and transformed into an essay on the meaning of war, memory and sacrifice.

The film combines violent war footage from the past with the somber present of the graves, the insane brutality of the killing with the eerie normality of present-day life. As in all of Brittain's films, the narration in FIELDS OF SACRIFICE does not describe what is being shown, but rather puts the images in context and heightens their impact. Here, Brittain collapses the past and present in a brilliant poetic counterpoint. In black and white, for example, we see a young soldier curled up dead on a beach in France, and then we cut to a colour image of the same beach with a modern-day sunbather curled up in the same position. Meanwhile, the narrator ironically suggests that we shall never forget the sacrifice of these soldiers.

Throughout his career, Brittain used narration freely and unabashedly for all of his documentaries and even many of his dramas. "Since they went to the trouble of inventing the talkies," he once said, "I figured I might as well make some noise." In Brittain's later work, narration delivered in the smokey growl of his own voice became a trademark, but in this early film his commentary is read by the actor Douglas Rain. In all of his films, Brittain's words are, in the truest sense, a revelation. They magically link disparate images and ideas. They are simple and direct, yet at the same time surprising and disturbing. Critics have talked about their "scorpion sting." Just as the audience is getting comfortable, Brittain hits them with something so strong that it wakes them up. Even on the printed page, the narration retains much of its power—the wit of conversation and the density of poetry. When a Donald Brittain film illuminates the screen, it is a lasting pleasure to listen to the writing.

"Monuments and men grow mellow and there are no longer friends and enemies...But only victims"

29

"You're like a guerilla platoon, you and the camera-man and the soundman..."

30

Narration from
Fields of Sacrifice

The ruins of Italy speak of them.
The poppies of Flanders stand for them.
They still echo across Vimy Ridge.
The flatlands of the Dutch can hear them.
They are the ghosts on the shores of France.
They haunt the sea off Normandy.
They have left their scars on the soil of Picardy.
They are remembered by the sand.
They live in the minds of old men who still travel
 the roads of the Somme.
They are the dead—the Canadian dead of the two
 World Wars—one hundred thousand of them.
They died in far places: places which still live and remember.

Hong Kong had seen them as fresh, unblooded troops.
 Then they heard: "the hills had got them."
Canadians, exhausted by the hills, attacked in the hills—
 killed in the beautiful hills of Hong Kong…
Places of defeat; places where they never stood a chance.
Buried with full honours, head to head, in the German style.

Memories over the gentle green heart of England.
Memories in the searing brown heart of Sicily.
Canadians moved through this cruel and alien land once,
 in a burning July.

The old people remember, for they had been starving and
 they were fed. And they heard stirring sounds of
 strange music. And they will tell the children.
An episode to be passed down, now part of the Sicilian
 legend of death, a part of the ancient land of blood.

The old man was watching them that morning.
Have a cup of coffee, his mother had called to them.
We did not know Canada was in the war.

They would never know such days again—these towns of
 Picardy. They made her famous with the song—she
 never understood the words, but she laughed along
 with them. For they would soon be dead.

The Canadian Memorials at Le Quesnel and
 Bourlong Wood.
The block of Canadian granite at Jury and
 Sanctuary Wood.
Passchendaele, where men choked to death on mud.
Courcelles, where men first saw the tank.
Saint Julien, where men first felt poison gas.

Time passes. Monuments and men grow mellow
 and there are no longer friends and enemies.
But only victims.

Bethune

1963
59 minutes

BETHUNE is Brittain's first biographical film, and one of his greatest. Like FIELDS OF SACRIFICE, it seemed like an impossible film to make. Norman Bethune died in China in 1940, leaving behind only letters, photographs, a scrap of movie film and a few friends and enemies in Canada. In China, he was carved into marble as a hero of the revolution; in Canada, until Brittain's film, few people had ever heard of him. It would be hard enough to make a written biography of such a man, but Brittain's task was much harder.

Nevertheless, Brittain made from these sparse elements a vivid portrait of this long-dead crusader; somehow, viewers of the film come to feel they know Bethune. At the heart of the film are Bethune's own words—letters to close friends which give us insights into the workings of his inner soul. Interviews with his wonderfully articulate associates and lovers add juicy tidbits: Bethune "thought he could smell a redhead." In the end, Brittain created a heroic character in the mold of Hemingway's fictional giants. Restless and passionate, articulate and rebellious, Brittain's Bethune charged at life full-tilt, taking life's pleasures with immense gusto and, with equal intensity, fighting to alleviate human suffering. But the film also makes Bethune a real person—haughty, selfish, authoritarian, yet impatient with authority, idealistic, hard drinking, womanizing—often a thoroughly unpleasant human being. All this, and at the same time a hero.

Brittain's Bethune charged at life full-tilt...

32

Brittain was fond of telling the story of how the making of this, one of the NFB's greatest films, was not officially approved by the Board. Even when completed, the head of the NFB tried to block its U.S. release. "In the end," Brittain said gleefully, "we knew that the Film Board had to back down because it was too embarrassing that Canadians couldn't export their heroes because the Americans objected to the fact that Bethune belonged to the Communist Party." In spite of the controversy, the film was an enormous success both in Canada and the United States. For the first time, Brittain got a taste of making films for a large audience. "It showed me the impact of film. If we had written the thing for Maclean's magazine it wouldn't have had one-tenth of the audience. When it ran on television, I saw the power of the medium and found it a bit scary. The responsibility became real—these were things that could affect a great number of people."

"In revolutionary friendship there is no distinction between Chinese and foreign."

*"The typewriter was one
of his few personal effects
and it always found a
place on the mules."*

34

Excerpts from

Bethune

Bethune: My father was an Evangelist, and
I come of a race of men violent, unstable,
of passionate convictions and wrong-
headedness, intolerant, yet with it all,
a vision of truth and a drive to carry
them on, even though it leads to their
own destruction.

Narration: *1926*—Bethune has tuberculosis
but his sense of fun never leaves him. He
predicts his date of death and decides to
go out laughing. There follow mad,
irreverent days and nights—parties with
nurses, neighbours and fellow patients.
And all this despite the fact that, not only
are they in the midst of a TB sanatorium,
they are in the midst of prohibition.

Interview: *With Dr. John Branwell.* He
considered himself a great judge of the
bootlegged whisky that might be brought
to us. He considered that it was not a fit
whiskey unless it could be drunk like
milk; and he prided himself that he
remembered the taste of both—good
whiskey and milk.

Narration: There is a rich man's tuberculosis and a poor man's tuberculosis. The rich man recovers, and the poor man dies. This succinctly expresses the close embrace of economics and pathology.

Bethune: *From a letter from Spain during the civil war.* We were heavily bombed today, about 12 noon. Standing in a doorway, as these huge machines flew slowly overhead, each one heavily loaded with bombs, I glanced up and down the street. A hush fell over the city—it was a hunted animal crouched down in the grass, quiet and apprehensive. There is no escape so be still. Then, in the dead silence of the street, the songs of birds came startling clear in the bright winter air.

If the building you happen to be in is hit, you will be killed or wounded. If it is not hit, you will not be killed or wounded. One place is really as good as another. After the bombs fall—and you can see them falling like great black pears—there is a thunderous roar. From heaps of huddled clothes on the cobblestones, blood begins to flow—these were once live women and children.

After the planes had passed, I picked up in my arms three dead children from the pavement where they had been standing in a great queue waiting for a cupful of preserved milk and a handful of dry bread. One's body felt as heavy as the dead themselves, but empty and hollow, and in one's brain burned a bright flame of hate.

I can't write you, my friends, as I should like to write you because my words are poor, anemic and hobbling things. "Uncomfortable?"—Good God!…

"Killed?"—for these poor huddled bodies of rags and blood, lying in such strange shapes, face down on the cobblestones, or with sightless eyes upturned to a cruel and indifferent sky. "Lovely?"—when the sun falls on our numbed faces like a benediction. So you see, it's no good.

Bethune: *From a letter from China.* Books? Are books still written? Is music still being played? Do you dance, drink beer, look at pictures? What do sheets in a soft bed feel like? Do women still love to be loved? Flora, I wish we had a radio and a hamburger sandwich…

Memorandum

1965
58 minutes

One of many films made about the Holocaust, MEMORANDUM still speaks to us today. In it, Brittain does not preach; he does not try to shock or moralize. In an almost bewildered voice, he merely asks how it could have happened. Or more specifically, how ordinary people could have allowed it to happen. Like FIELDS OF SACRIFICE, MEMORANDUM is a haunting contrast of past with present—of memory with what is happening now. When it was released, this film was not only a powerful statement but also a superb technical achievement. It was Brittain's first film to use the new portable camera techniques successfully. The cinéma verité part of the film covers the voyage of a survivor of Bergen-Belsen, Bernard Laufer, as he returns to show the camp to his teenage son.

Brittain's genius was to take this event and link it to an extraordinary series of inquiries. His aim was to make the events of the genocide comprehendable, to show how they fit within human experience. As the film unfolds, Laufer tries to convey to his son the enormity of the Holocaust. Instead, he and the audience are confronted with a contented and affluent Germany. Banality is mixed with evil, the ordinary with the unthinkable. Life goes on; even the death camp has become a pleasant green park. "Nobody knows," murmurs Laufer, shaking his head. "Nobody knows," echoes the narration.

"…20 years after…How much has already been forgotten?"

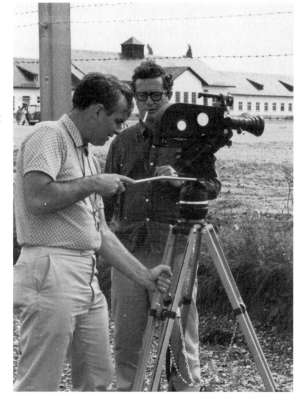

The deeper message of MEMORANDUM is summarized by the contemporary German playwright Peter Weiss, who at the time was producing a play about the concentration camps. His play, he notes, "is dedicated to the notion that once a crime has been committed it becomes a potentiality for all time." The film does not present any new information to the observer of the contemporary world, only a reminder—a memorandum.

Narration from

Memorandum

Early one morning in Munich in the summer of 1965. In a few days, Fraulein Mara Bellett will be celebrating her twenty-fourth birthday. She was born in 1941—the year that Hitler decided, among other things, that she should never see a Jew. But that's finished now, and there's enough to do, getting ready for the day ahead.

In Dachau, for the first time, doctors were able to conduct what they called 'terminal' experiments such as this gradual withdrawal of oxygen. Dachau opened in 1933. But the world had seen concentration camps before. In 1936, Hitler really opened the eyes of the world. There had never been super-highways like his autobahns.

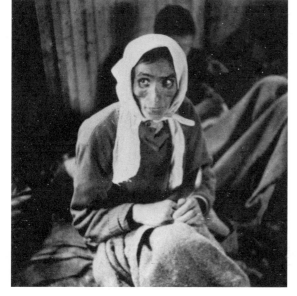

"...once a crime has been committed
it becomes a potentiality for all time."

37

Then one night in 1938, Jewish property across Germany was demolished. Many Germans were embarrassed. One told a *Life* magazine reporter, "Don't look," he said, "this isn't the real Germany…." Then Hitler announced that war would bring the annihilation of the European Jew. It was assumed that this was a figure of speech.

And that very day in 1965, some of the men responsible are on trial in Frankfurt. Here they come now: seventeen of them, late of the Auschwitz administration. Some killed with gas and needle and club. And some with the pointing of a finger. Maltke, the adjutant, who kept track of things, and then went into the export trade. Capesius, the druggist, who helped in eight thousand murders, but said he was always polite. Papa Kaduk, who sat in his chapel, and admitted he occasionally had to pull himself together. Doctor Klehr, who punctured hearts with a needle, and Bednarek, who interrupted torture for prayer, and Wilhelm Boger, who beat men's testicles until they died.

Boger, Kuduk and four others get the maximum sentence—life at hard labour. Most of the rest get lighter terms. Three are acquitted, for it is murder which must be proved. Shobert, the Gestapo representative: "I killed no one personally," he tells the court, and they let him go.

They rejoin the German crowd. And who will ever know who murdered by memorandum, who did the filing and the typing from nine o'clock to five, with an hour off for lunch.

And if it could happen in the fairyland of Hansel and Gretel, and the Pied Piper of Hamelin, could it not happen anywhere?

And could it not happen anywhere, if it could happen in the cultured land of Bach, Beethoven and Schiller?

And how could it happen in a land of churches? There were some martyrs, it's true—but where were the other servants of Christ?

And where were the scholars of Heidelberg? They were with the captains of industry and among the first to play along.

And how could it all have started in the happy land of Bavaria? In this, the Hofbrau House of Munich, Adolph Hitler first laid out his program to the world. But why should that darken the festive summer night? A third of them are tourists, a third were too young and the other third is sick and tired of the whole business.

An old German says, we are a cursed generation. Not just us but some of you too. We will take our horrible place in history. Can you just let us quietly live out our time? There is really nothing anyone can do.

Never a Backward Step

1966
57 minutes

With this portrait of Canadian newspaper baron Lord Thomson of Fleet, Brittain perfected his biographical story-telling technique. Television biography, particularly of famous people, is often predictable, superficial and, in the end, curiously unrevealing. A Brittain portrait is the opposite. It gives you the dates and the main points, but also all the telling details that the official portraits so often leave out—the great stories, the twitches and mannerisms, the inconsistencies and gossip that in the end reveal the essence of the subject.

Lord Thomson was a small-town businessman from Northern Ontario who ended up owning more newspapers than any other man in the world. His empire included radio and television stations and a few publishing houses. Brittain got his permission to follow him around for a few days. During this time, we see the many sides of Roy Thomson—from the empire-building businessman to the visitor in a grade school classroom instructing the kids to mind their sums. Throughout the movie, Brittain plays on the irony of this petty, small-town, awkward man socializing with prime ministers and intellectuals. We watch him being fitted out with his robes for the House of Lords, worrying about whether they will be able to be

Lord Thomson of Fleet.

shortened for use by his son. We see him scribbling numbers on bits of paper and compulsively scratching them out. We hear the story of this multi-millionaire happily taking advantage of a free bus trip to Northern Ireland and disappearing in the afternoon to buy another paper for his empire—*The Belfast Telegraph.*

These little moments add up to an appreciation of this strange man. He is not a bad person, although you know he can be ruthless; he is sometimes foolish, although certainly no fool; he is pompous, but genuinely humble. In the end, Brittain managed to capture on film a very ordinary Canadian, who through luck and dogged hard work became one of the most powerful men in the world.

...These little moments add up to an appreciation of this strange man...

"Lord Thomson: Colonel-in-Chief of the Toronto Scottish Regiment and very ordinary Canadian."

Narration from
Never A Backward Step

Narration: His 35,000 employees include some of the finest journalists in the world. Yet he describes news as "the stuff you put between the ads," and a television license as "a license to print money."

Interview: *With a British reporter.* There is a curious succession of waves of Canadian bruisers who come over to the British Press—you know Lord Beaverbrook and that lot—and because we're so badly set up and because we don't know what we're protecting anyway, they can go—phut—through it just like that. Then a funny little thing happens: the British fall over backwards and thank them very much for it. There is a funny kind of way in which we like the colonial to come in and be tough and beat up our press for us. If an Englishman did it, they'd call it vulgar.

Narration: Thomson bought his first newspaper, *The Timmins Press*, in 1934. It is still making money for him in Northern Ontario.

Narration: The son of a Toronto barber, he headed north in 1928. He wanted to sell radios, but there wasn't a station; so he started one. The North Bay merchants bought up air time…and Thomson began to build a string of small-town enterprises. Soon he was saying that the sweetest music in the world was the sound of a spot commercial at ten bucks a whack.

Interview: *With Albert MacKay, a newspaper editor in Scotland whom Thomson had fired.* Well, it was handled pleasantly, but it was still a shock. I am sure that as far as Roy Thomson was concerned, it was as pulling your teeth is to many a dentist—it was an entirely painless extraction; but it wasn't painless to me. My wife had prepared for my lunch that day, a haggis. She still had it in the pot when I came home for lunch. When I told her, the shock was so big that the haggis never came out of the pot. So I've always said that last Saturday was the day our haggis died.

Narration: Thomson's wife died in 1951 and he lives alone. But in a deeper sense, he has always been alone. As a boy, he was half-blind and ungainly. As a man, he has locked himself up in his work. If, as some say, he is incomplete and one-dimensional, he is certainly not in the least unhappy. He enjoys the company of successful men, but even in a crowd, he is essentially alone.

Brittain plays on the irony of this…man.

41

Volcano:
An Inquiry into the Life and Death of Malcolm Lowry
1976
99 minutes

Whereas films like BETHUNE, NEVER A BACKWARD STEP and LADIES AND GENTLEMEN, LEONARD COHEN present wonderfully complex portraits of their subjects, VOLCANO takes film biography one step further. This 99-minute impressionistic rumination on the life of the alcoholic author Malcolm Lowry is nothing less than an X-ray of a man's soul. In form, it is neither documentary nor drama, but an extraordinary hybrid—a new type of filmmaking invented by Brittain to tell this story. VOLCANO is his masterpiece.

"Brittain always made sure that the people who worked with him got as involved with the subject as he did," says Volcano's producer, Robert Duncan. "We worked for several years on the film, and during that time there was not one day when we didn't talk about Malcolm Lowry. We quoted him to each other, drew parallels between our lives, looked for omens and talked to the dead man as if he was still with us. Lowry became our daily bread, but it was Brittain who was the baker."

Malcolm Lowry was one of the great literary geniuses of our age, but he wrote only one book worth reading. It took him eight

years to do it, and the process destroyed him. Haunted by homosexuality, guilt and paranoia, Lowry's life was a downward spiral of impotence, alcoholism and, ultimately, insanity. The film tells this story in two ways: from the inside, through Lowry's own tortured words, read by Richard Burton, and from the outside, through interviews with friends and family who helplessly watched his self-destruction.

The interviews are remarkable. There is Lowry's brother, who pours out years of pent-up frustration over living with this irresponsible and embarrassing family legend. There is Lowry's psychiatrist, who describes the treatment he gave Lowry to cure him of alcoholism—a program which bordered on torture. Then there is a school chum, now an old man, who remembers Lowry as someone who could fart at will. Finally, there is Lowry's long-suffering wife, who describes the sad details of their poisoned, blessed life together.

Lowry's novel, UNDER THE VOLCANO, is set in Cuernevaca, Mexico during the Day of the Dead. The film's grotesque footage of present-day Mexico echoes the words of Lowry's book, giving them a new and strange dimension. These are not literal images to illustrate the words—instead we see Lowry's "Mexico of the heart" in the ineradicable images of a nightmare.

VOLCANO was a very special film for Brittain. As if to underline his affinity for his subject, near the beginning of the film we see the startling image of Brittain emptying a bottle of beer over Lowry's grave. "I am a member of the great brotherhood of alcohol," Brittain said to an interviewer after the film's release. "People used to say that I was bent on the same sort of thing and

...Lowry's life was a downward spiral...

maybe for a while I was. I was caught up in the romanticization of self-destruction, but I managed to survive, and he didn't."

"In this film, I have tried to get inside the head of a man who is supersensitive, who is beset by many demons. I've tried to look out at the world from his point of view. He was a man of genius and of incredible weakness. But because he was a man of weakness, he was a man of great courage. He poured himself into this one great book and obtained salvation through his work. But I think he knew when he had finished his book, he had finished himself."

...a man who is supersensitive, who is beset by demons.

44

Narration from
Volcano

Narration: On the Day of the Dead, November 2, 1936, Mr. and Mrs. Malcolm Lowry arrived in Mexico. Lowry was 27 years of age. His passport described him as a writer, but he considered his only book an embarrassment. His life, in fact, was an embarrassment.

[His wife] Jan Gabriel was not spending too much time with Malcolm Lowry. She was sure that she had married a genius but that genius seemed largely bent on self-destruction. At any rate, they settled in a small house on the Calle Humbolt…Here he began to write a book he called UNDER THE VOLCANO. Gradually a creature that Lowry called simply the Consul began to emerge. Miraculously, for he was still drinking as heavily as ever and his marriage was in shreds, Lowry began to write as he had never written before. Perhaps this was his last hope—the justification and redemption of his largely worthless life, for the Consul who drinks mescal down to the worm is not a creature of fiction at all, but Malcolm Lowry himself.

Reading: *From UNDER THE VOLCANO,* Oozing alcohol from every pore, the Consul stood at the open door of the salon Ophelia. How sensible to have had a mescal, how sensible.

Narration: Lowry was writing about a defrocked British diplomat in the final stages of alcoholic disintegration. He was also writing, sometimes with good humour, about Hell.

Reading: But look here, hang it all, it is not altogether darkness. You misunderstand me if you think it is altogether darkness I see… But, if you look at that sunlight there then perhaps you'll get the answer. See, look—look at the way it falls through the window. What beauty can compare to that of the cantina in the early morning. Not even the gates of Heaven opening wide to receive me could fill me with such celestial, complicated and hopeless joy as the iron screen that rolls up with a crash!…All mystery, all hopes, all disappointment, yes all disaster is there beyond those swinging doors.

45

Henry Ford's America

1976
57 minutes

Made in the same year as the brooding, sombre VOLCANO, HENRY FORD'S AMERICA is light, wry and highly entertaining. Brittain's assignment was to make a film illustrating the impact of the automobile on society. The film does this admirably, but not as a sociological thesis. "When I undertook the project," said Brittain, "I realized that there had been thousands of films made about the automobile. So I decided to personalize my film by looking at one man who stood at the center of the car industry."

The person is Henry Ford II, heir and absolute dictator of the Ford empire. Interviewed by Brittain, Ford tells a revealing story about trying to break through the picket lines during a strike at his grandfather's factory by roaring up the Rouge River in a speedboat. "I thought it'd be kind of fun, you know—I was young and I didn't give a damn."

The film paints a vivid picture of the combat zone this former playboy created in his upper management. We get a glimpse of Lee Iacocca, then Ford Vice-President and creator of the Mustang, who tells us he likes men with fire in their belly.

...Henry Ford gave us the Model-T, exhaust fumes (and) the consumers movement...

Brittain prophetically notes that the Ford Motor Company has the highest executive mortality rate in the industry. Soon after this film was made, and without explanation, Henry Ford II abruptly fired Iacocca, the most successful of his young executives.

Ford's grandfather was equally ruthless, but he was the man who turned the toy of the rich into a birthright of the American masses. Much of the film examines with amused fascination the enormous hold that Ford's creation has had on the public. There is the preacher of the drive-in church, for example, who finds the car an excellent space in which to contemplate the hereafter; there is

"He is the last of the great dynastic chiefs. Each man is here at his pleasure..."

the customizer who regards it as a medium for artistic expression; and there are people like Mandy Pearson for whom the car is life itself. We learn that she earns $100 a week and spends $40 on gasoline. She describes how someone once backed into her beloved Mustang and she sat sobbing in the back of the police car, "'Cause it hurt my car and it hurt me at the same time."

HENRY FORD'S AMERICA is a truly fun film, a realization of Brittain's ambition to make documentaries as entertaining as a Cary Grant film. Brittain plays the car culture for all it is worth, but at the same time he views its excesses with ironic detachment. Because of this invention, he reminds us, more people have been slaughtered on the road than in all of America's wars. But then, he impishly adds, an equal number have probably been conceived in its back seat.

47

Narration from
Henry Ford's America

Two million Americans have died in it. Although comparative figures are not readily available, it's estimated that about the same number have been conceived in it. It is therefore fair to say that it brings out the best and the worst in man.

The age of the automobile has been dated from 1926 when it was first reported that Americans had more cars than bathtubs. But then, you can't go to town in a bathtub.

On the 12th floor of world headquarters, Henry Ford II had a president and 45 assorted vice-presidents… It is not easy to reach the 12th floor, and the stay can be depressingly short. There is a file on each of a thousand executives. On each man's file, it is said, there are the names of three men who could replace him. Each executive is colour-coded. They can be green, blue, yellow or red. A red will soon be out of work, a green is a man with a future.

The Ford Motor Company has another distinction. There's no Mr. General Motors, there's not even a Mr. Chrysler anymore, but there is a Mr. Ford. His occasional fondness for strong drink and his difficulties with wives and traffic cops has created some confusion in the minds of laymen as to whether or not he actually goes to work. There is no such confusion in the House of Ford. He is the last of the great dynastic chiefs. Each man is here at his pleasure, invited to come and advise him in the monastic secrecy of the Design Center.

Once upon a time design meetings were unnecessary. Old Henry the First offered a single model, and if you wanted any colour but black, you had to paint it yourself. When Henry the Second was born in 1917, his grandfather had just finished trying to stop the First World War. It was the only thing that he tried that hadn't worked…He introduced the moving assembly line, which cut the cost dramatically, and the toy of the European rich became the birthright of the American masses. It was cheap, durable and easy to fix. Precisely right for a restless migrant population trying to fill up a huge, undeveloped continent. Henry Ford had made America free to move.

Down through the generations, it has indeed been the teenager who has best understood the deeper meanings of the motoring age. For they were the first to realize the possibilities of the rumble seat and to discover the irresistible mating call of the motoring horn. A cornerstone of American morality—the difficulty of finding a suitable place for misconduct—

had been forever blown away. Here at last was a private place that could be moved at will to quiet country lanes. Even the moon could be manoeuvered into place and with a little ingenuity and suppleness of limb all things at last were possible.

To some men a place to meet with God. To others an instrument of the devil. A simple machine that seems to defy description. But whatever it is, Henry Ford plans to keep on making it until such time as America decides on some other form of civilization.

"It was cheap, durable and easy to fix...Henry Ford had made America free to move."

Paperland: The Bureaucrat Observed

1979
58 minutes

B rittain called this film his "office boy's revenge." He loved the National Film Board for the support and freedom it gave him, but he often watched with horror as it aimlessly spun its bureaucratic wheels, churning previously creative filmmakers into paper pushers. A risk-taker throughout his life, Brittain despised those who opted for the comfortable collectivity of large organizations. He himself left the Board at the peak of his success and remained a freelancer for the rest of his career.

PAPERLAND is unusual because it is an 'idea' film, a film not with a particular person but with an idea—bureaucracy—as its focus. Although a film with a serious message, in form it remains light, quirky and surprising.

The film takes the viewer around the world—to Ottawa of course, but also to a Caribbean island of only 230 people, home of the world's smallest bureaucracy; to the Vatican, the world's oldest bureaucracy; and to Marxist Hungary, to show how the absurdities of the bureaucracy can flourish under every political system. The idea may be abstract, but Brittain still revels in the human particulars.

PAPERLAND shows us pensioners in Hungary pleading with government officials to get the elevator in their building working; moving day at Statistics Canada when civil servants rise up in arms

against the loss of their office doors; a Government of Canada official taxidermist, who may not stuff a bear until its papers are in order; the solitary bureaucrat on the tiny island who literally wears different hats to carry out his various functions as postmaster, tax collector and census taker; and an anonymous papal functionary who adds his comments to a memo dated 1643.

This film is an example of Brittain's ability to bring a complex subject down to earth. The countless small examples build until we begin to realize the essential irrationality of a system that can take intelligent individuals and cause them to commit collective absurdities. Brittain himself was not unaware of the irony of biting the bureaucratic hand that paid his filmmaking bills. "I guess I'm considered a double-crosser," he said in an interview after the film's stormy release. "I'm considered part of the establishment who is airing dirty linen in public and not playing the game. But what the hell, if you're going to play the game, you're finished."

Brittain himself was not unaware of the irony...

51

Narration from

Paperland

Here he comes now, trying to act like a normal human being. But he is the most despised of human creatures. His activities have brought down upon his shoulders the scorn and outrage of history's multitudes. He is 'homo bureaucratis', the bureaucrat, and he lives in the land of paper.

He has been compared to the cockroach. Like the cockroach, he appears to have no useful function. Like the cockroach, he has many enemies. Like the cockroach, he has survived all attempts at extermination.

Bureaucrats were first seen standing by the canal builders of ancient Egypt, filling out the forms. Behind each stonemason in the Great Wall of China stood a bureaucrat with a requisition. The more complex the undertaking, the greater the need for paper work, and thus, in the monumental confusion of the twentieth century, we have finally come to the golden age of bureaucracy.

The castle of Louden, in the Vienna Woods, has a typical history. It failed as a castle. It failed as a hotel. But it flourishes as a finishing school for bureaucrats. And how will these young bureaucrats be ultimately judged? They will not be judged on whether or not they have promoted truth over falsehood, love over hate, joy over despair. They will be judged solely on whether or not they have followed the proper procedure.

The bureaucrat lives in an unnatural state. To do his job properly he should rid himself of passion, initiative and common sense. What remains, according to one sociologist, is the truncated remnant of a human being.

Newly elected heads of state invariably promise that they will cut the civil service. Pierre Elliott Trudeau, on becoming Prime Minister of Canada, vowed that he would reduce the civil service by 25,000 jobs. Now, as he whiles away his last hours after 11 years of power, he may notice that he is surrounded by 40,000 more bureaucrats than when he came to office. He may also notice that they are still working, while he has lost his job.

A public bureaucracy is filled with good intentions and boundless energy. Where its goals are simple, such as putting a man on the moon, or transporting Jews to gas ovens, it works with relentless efficiency. But where the goals are complex and contradictory, it begins to move in never-ending aimless circles. Perhaps we should be grateful for this confusion. The only thing that saves us from bureaucratic subjugation is the inertia of the bureaucracy itself.

In the end, we, the people, and they, the bureaucrats, at least share in one common feeling—complete helplessness. Here in a basement in Budapest, the circle is complete. Retired public servants, after a lifetime of administering the rules, come to a special place for help through their own last bits of red tape.

On some not-too-distant day, we will perhaps all be gathered around one glorious table, attending the ultimate meeting, a sort of 'committee of all mankind', having long since forgotten what the meeting was all about.

The Champions

1978 & 1986
Part I: 57 minutes
Part II: 56 minutes
Part III: 87 minutes

Brittain was once asked why he slaved so hard over his films. "It's my life," he answered: "this is what I'm going to leave behind. You pick timeless subjects and treat them properly, and people are going to be looking at them two hundred years from now. We are stockpiling history. The portraits of the twentieth century are documentary films. Instead of looking at faces hanging in a gallery somewhere, you're going to be watching a movie about them."

Throughout his long career, in one way or another, Brittain was always painting a portrait of Canada. In this series, he finally discovered a way of dealing with issues which go to the very core of Canada's survival. He found his story in the curiously interlocking careers of Pierre Eliott Trudeau and René Lévesque, a tale of two ideologues filled with fire and passion and very different views of the destiny of the nation.

The raw material for THE CHAMPIONS was the stuff we have all seen before—the news reports, the interviews and the stock footage. Brittain's genius, in this mammoth three-and-a-half-hour compilation, was to fit all the pieces together—to make sense of it all. What resulted was "a drama as taut as the best fictional political thriller," according to a critic from *Variety*.

"They are...prisoners of each other..."

"If anyone wanted to give an outsider a crash course on Canada," he added, "these films would suffice in explaining all about the complexities and eccentricities of the two solitudes."

"From time immemorial the champion of a cause, its defender on the final battleground was its fiercest and most noble warrior." So begins Brittain's narration, and as the films unfold, we begin to understand the men beneath the warriors' armour and, through them, our history. Adam Symansky, who produced THE CHAMPIONS: THE FINAL BATTLE, explains that "Brittain was never interested in the mechanics of what was going on—the Referendum—that was sheer drudgery for him—the Constitution— oh God. What he was interested in was what was going on in their hearts while these other things were going on." One of the ways THE CHAMPIONS reveals the interior of the two men is by using outtakes captured by the cameras before and after the politicians were officially 'on'.

"Lévesque had in his possession the awesome weapons of office."

Brittain is describing a great political passion play, a time of strong personalities and deeply felt principles. Looking at the personalities and passions of leaders today, it seems by comparison that, in Trudeau's parlance, the pipsqueaks are running the world. For many viewers, seeing these films in the 1990s will be a nostalgic experience. Where in the Canadian political landscape, in this homogenized era of the bland, are today's champions?

The dry words of Brittain's citation for the Order of Canada pay tribute to his "masterful visual records of our social and cultural past." THE CHAMPIONS is such a record, one of the most important that Brittain made; a film that will outlive its protagonists.

Narration from

The Champions

Part I: Unlikely Warriors

Lévesque…lived in a remote little town on the Gaspe coast. Although New Carlisle was largely English and the English had most of the money, this fact did not leave any permanent scars on René Lévesque. He himself will tell you that he had a very good time. The French and the English called each other names, punched each other out and then played together in the snow.

Trudeau spent eight years at Brebeuf College. It was run by the Jesuits and it was dedicated to the fine-tuning of the human mind. It was a world of logic and reason, uncluttered by the passions and emotions of the world outside.

…A tale of two ideologues filled with fire and passion…

Part II: Trappings Of Power

Pierre Trudeau was Canada's third bachelor prime minister but neither MacKenzie King or R.B. Bennett ever went out with girls like Barbara Streisand. He was the first prime minister of Canada who was more famous than the prime minister of England.

If he was the most intelligent prime minister since Arthur Meighen, he was also the most removed and solitary. Isolated by a computer and a small palace guard, access to the seat of power was limited to that handful of senior civil servants, the legendary mandarins of Ottawa.

In 1972, he called an election, announced that the land was strong, and declined to campaign. His Cartesian logic and Socratic dialogues did not go down well in a Drummondville cafeteria. He offered Quebec little, but enough of them voted for him to save him from political oblivion. He was more in his element with the great men and issues of the time. Here he could realize his dream of Canada moving with stature through the international community. Lévesque had called him a citizen, not of Quebec, or of Canada, but of the world.

Part III: The Final Battle

November 15th, 1976...Lévesque's astounding victory must have been the dark moment in Pierre Trudeau's political life. By achieving power, the cause of separation had taken a quantum leap. The movement was now credible. It had a momentum and Levesque had in his possession the awesome weapons of office.

In the aftermath of the election, the Royal 22nd Regiment stood firm at the Citadel, but a lot of other people didn't know if they were coming or going. They set tables in New York to listen to Lévesque, who claimed he was George Washington. Then Trudeau came to the States and claimed he was Abraham Lincoln. The Americans were confused.

Neither man entered politics until he was in middle life, but such is their impact that they seem to have been around for ever. Neither man sought power, but it came to them. It is not really a battle between the emotional and the rational man; both minds are brilliant, both souls are passionate and there is a fine rage in each. Both are glad that, at last, it has come to this time of confrontation. They are, in a sense, prisoners of each other and this will be their final battle.

"Neither man sought power, but it came to them."

Canada's Sweetheart: The Saga of Hal C. Banks

1985
115 minutes

CANADA'S SWEETHEART is the story of Hal Banks, a gangster imported into Canada to crush the Communist-controlled Canadian Seamen's Union. With guns, baseball bats and government complicity, Banks succeeded in bringing a more compliant union to the Great Lakes. In the process, he destroyed the careers of over six thousand seamen. This powerful story, based on court transcripts, is told through dramatic recreation intercut with startling documentary interviews with actual victims of Banks' 20-year reign of terror.

This marriage of documentary realism with dramatic recreations is called reality television today, but in one way or another, Brittain had been experimenting with this hybrid art form since the beginning of his career. As he himself pointed out, "Any difference between documentary, docu-drama and drama doesn't have much significance. Documentaries also manipulate material." In CANADA'S SWEETHEART, Brittain combines the strengths of both forms of filmmaking. As critic Rick Groen said, "for once the devices of fiction serve to clarify—not distort—the din of fact."

"Sometimes I haven't had time to be a gentleman."

Brittain had directed for the CBC before making CANADA'S SWEETHEART, and had experimented with simple recreations in the NFB/CBC series ON GUARD FOR THEE (1981). But this film was Brittain's first major success with drama. CANADA'S SWEETHEART was a success partly because it tells a good story with a strong central character—Maury Chaykin's depiction of Hal Banks as a muscle-bound sleaze is very convincing. But in this film Brittain also perfected his technique of 'narrated drama'. The narration is the glue that tells some of the story and links the dramatic scenes. Interspersed are documentary interviews that jolt the viewer out of the drama and back to the realization that this is not a piece of fantasy—that those were real heads being smashed.

Brittain never treated film as a platform from which to spout his ideologies, but in this film he reveals some of his own convictions. In conversation, Brittain frequently raged against that peculiar brand of Canadian smugness which hides its hypocrisy behind the banner of "peace, order, and good government." Apart from Hal Banks, the real villain in CANADA'S SWEETHEART is the Canadian government, which imported Banks, quietly condoned his brutality and then, for 25 years, protected him from prosecution. In among the cracked heads and punctured kidneys of the victims, the film features a grinning, real-life ex-Cabinet Minister, Jack Pickersgill, stroking his poodle while waffling thin excuses. In Brittain's hands, documentary can be more grotesque than fiction.

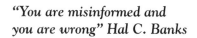

"You are misinformed and you are wrong" **Hal C. Banks**

Excerpts from
Canada's Sweetheart

Narration: Because of him, men once feared to walk the streets. A judge once called him a 'Frankenstein monster', a fellow union leader called him a psychopathic brute. And yet, when he got himself in trouble, cabinet ministers rushed to his defense. One minister said it was rather fun having our own gangster. He was Hal C. Banks, and in the 1950s he was as famous as Barbara Ann Scott.

Interview: *With Jimmy Todd, an elected S.I.U. union leader who fought Banks' absolute rule. He is talking about some goons who had appeared at the door of his house.*

Todd: I think that in their mind they were told I was living alone at the time because my wife had just returned from Scotland where we had to send her to keep her out of trouble at the beginning. And I suppose they didn't realize that she was there. So I started to get into a little argument, and at that point the wife Agnes came out of the kitchen and says…

Agnes Todd: I had just put Patricia in her high chair. I didn't want her to get underneath their feet so I harnessed her in her high chair…So I lifted a pot of hot fat off the stove and went in and I said, "Are your friends staying for supper, Jim?" And he said, "They're no friends of mine." And I said, "Well in that case

they'll be leaving." Actually it was a Friday night and we always have fish and French fries on Friday nights so it was a convenient time. Oh yes, they left almost immediately. It was good and hot…

Narration: Dick Greaves had also decided to take his chances. He had been double-crossed. Banks had made a move to take over Greaves's union. On the East Coast the marine engineers had been raided by Banks…

Greaves: We were doing some work in the afternoon and there was a knock at the door. They said, "We came to give you something," and they caught me in the temple.

Brittain: If somebody is coming after you, you always put your back to the wall—is that what you try to do, you try to land on your back?

Greaves: Back, right! Or land on your back because, you know, if they kick you, they're going to kick your kidneys in. If they kick you in the ribs, well that's one thing. It's sort of hollow and bouncy, but if they get a good real solid kick into your kidneys, well, it'll dislodge the damn things from inside and you'll probably have real trouble all the rest of your life.

Re-creation: *Bank's hearing at the Norris Commission.*

Charles Dubin, lawyer for the Commission: Are you saying to me that the people who came to this commission and said they were beaten up had not been beaten up?

Hal Banks: I would say that some of them weren't. And I would say that some of them were psychopaths, and I would put them in that category with respect to the question as to who beat them up.

Dubin: We know and we have the evidence of a Captain Bissette, who has been an employee of Upper Lakes for many years…

Banks: I don't know what the hell they were…bar room brawls or what they were…

Dubin: He was beaten up at a department store.

Banks: I have seen captains beat up and I have seen captains beat people up several times in my career on the waterfront. There could be a hundred reasons for it. I have seen captains running out of an apartment house with an irate husband at their necks etcetera, I don't see how the S.I.U. could have been involved in this. You are misinformed and you are wrong.

Justice Norris: Harold C. Banks is capable, decisive, egocentric, intolerant and ruthless. He is of the stuff of the Capones and the Hoffas. He is a bully—cruel, dishonest, greedy, power-hungry and contemptuous of the law.…In this generally law-abiding country, where we boast of our culture and our freedom, decent citizens were afraid to walk the streets and afraid to take the stand in support of their rights. Witnesses came to give evidence still bearing the marks of beating. Some were crippled or marked for life.

And what are we to say of those who supported and protected him here and in the United States? Respected businessmen, labour leaders and above all politicians. They have no such justifying circumstances in their upbringing and yet they aided and abetted him at every turn, and thus share in the responsibility for his crimes.

"…it was rather fun having our own gangster."

The King Chronicle

1987
Part 1: 100 minutes
Part 2: 105 minutes
Part 3: 103 minutes

Brittain loved challenges. "It is no fun to win," he once told a colleague, "unless you're coming from behind." In this six-hour portrait of William Lyon Mackenzie King, Brittain had perhaps found his greatest challenge. On a technical level alone, it was a major feat. Brittain tells a story that began in the nineteenth century and ended in the middle of the twentieth. Cars, fashions, military uniforms and interior decor had to be accurate if the drama was to work. Added to this were dozens of complex locations and a 90-member cast, all to be assembled on a shoestring budget. The final achievement is all the more remarkable when we realize this was the first drama in which Brittain did not rely on documentary intervention. There are no interviews with real characters; the film is written from beginning to end.

The greatest challenge, however, was presented by the film's subject. "Making films about Bethune and Trudeau was a lot easier," Brittain acknowledged. "They are up-front, macho stuff. Mackenzie King is the antithesis of confrontation and drama.

"I don't think the man was capable of compromise."

He waffled, appeased, compromised and deliberately bored people to death. Any drama there is was inside."

Mackenzie King was a subject who almost imposed himself on Brittain. Like most Canadians, Brittain had never liked the man. Growing up in Ottawa, he had looked on him as a national embarrassment sitting beside the Churchills and the Roosevelts of the world. But since Brittain had made so many movies about recent Canadian history, King was an unavoidable presence. There he was lurking in the background of the CANADA AT WAR series, and of the Gouzenko spy case in ON GUARD FOR THEE. In fact, through almost 50 years of history, according to Brittain, he was always there, "the embodiment of many of the contradictions that underlie the querulous nature of what it is to be Canadian." In the film Brittain quotes historian Bruce Hutchison: "If we don't understand King, we don't understand ourselves."

"It is, of course, the darker side of ourselves," Brittain explained, "the embodiment of that unsavory element in this country, a wildly exaggerated need for security and respectability. King, in his hypocrisy, always gave Canadians the easy way out. He was the great conciliator, a leader in constant search of the path of least resistance. He never challenged us as a nation."

In making the film, the trick was to make the great conciliator into a character able to hold an audience for six hours. It would have been easy to take cheap shots; to paint King, with his adored mother, his sainted dogs and his crystal ball, as a sanctimonious fool. Instead, Brittain took his subject seriously and probed behind the bland public image. His major weapon was King's own twelve million word personal diary. King, the most

secretive of men, used his diary as an alter ego, and into it he poured all of his rationalizations, his vanity and his musings about the supernatural. The diary gives the film its historical validity and it provides that window which Brittain always looked for, the window into the inner life of his subject.

Did Brittain succeed in nailing down King as he had done with Bethune and Trudeau? "In the end I had trouble drawing conclusions," Brittain was finally to admit. "In the end, all I could do was to let the audience come in as a private secretary to Mackenzie King and be privy to all the things in the back corner. Let them draw their own conclusions." In fact, people who had known and had worked with King were startled by the realism of Brittain's portrait. He succeeded in capturing, if not explaining, this enigmatic Canadian to a large television audience.

King, Roosevelt and Churchill
"He was the great conciliator,
a leader in constant search of
the path of least resistance."

The *Globe and Mail* summed up the film and its anti-hero this way: "In Brittain's talented hands, King becomes an eccentric tea cozy of a man, a fussy old asexual nutcake who seems to trip pigeon-toed through history like a dear maiden aunt. His renowned political acuity and ruthlessness become clear only in the turn of events, comprehensible because of Brittain's orderly and entertaining narration. Somehow, THE KING CHRONICLE is a triumph in spite of its subject."

King was devastated when his dog died...

Excerpts from

The King Chronicles

Part I: Mackenzie King and the Unseen Hand
A creature who cast no shadow, though he ruled the land of the midnight sun.

A summer's day in Ottawa, 1909. A time to discuss the new trophy Lord Grey is donating for football, or the heartwarming success of a new book, Anne of Green Gables; a moment of relaxation for the two men who will dominate the Dominion of Canada for half a century. The one with the white hair is Sir Wilfrid Laurier, a fine figure of a man. The fatter person is Mr. Mackenzie King, who is often compared to a toad. When their statues are built, Sir Wilfrid's will stand noble in the sunlight. Mr. King, on the other hand, will stand in perpetual gloom beside a parking lot.

Part II: Mackenzie King and the Great Beyond
Franklin Roosevelt gave men hope and did everything he could to give them jobs. When he spoke of a rendezvous with destiny, he inspired a generation. In Canada there was silence. Eight hundred thousand Canadians had no jobs; thousands more had no homes. Capitalism had failed. Nature itself had failed. The wheat fields had blown away. The Prairie farmers ate dust and called out to heaven for bread.

Mackenzie King seemed to have been born for this moment. Here was a trained economist. Here was the man who had once written that industry must have a human heart, that government must be the guardian of the oppressed. But when he was needed most, he proved to be an unctuous fraud. He didn't know what the Depression was all about. And he didn't seem to care. He wandered fussily through his phoney ruins. It was a good place for him. His mind was encrusted with nineteenth century platitudes, his compassion confined to friends and acquaintances. He was very kind to dogs.

Part III: Mackenzie King and the Zombie Army

If Mackenzie King had his way, the Second World War would never have happened. Goodness knows, he'd done everything to avoid it. Mr. King was a master of appeasement—a handmaiden of Neville Chamberlain. Peace at any cost. It was not that he was a pacifist or had a morbid fear of Hitler. He was afraid of what Canadians might do to each other. Since he had first taken office, he had been busy trying to keep Canada from coming apart at the seams. The French Catholic Church and much of Quebec favoured the Fascists; much of Ontario would ride into the valley of death for the British. Then there was the Ku Klux Klan, a Communist Party, a Nazi Party, funny money in Alberta and Socialists in Saskatchewan. All the elements of the great dominion rattled around in Mackenzie King, which might account both for his chronic indigestion and his political invincibility.

William Lyon Mackenzie King
"He waffled, appeased, compromised
and deliberately bored people to death."

Filmography

Filmography

1954

Canadian Profile
National Film Board of Canada
Location Manager

A coast-to-coast survey of how industrialization affects the lives of 'ordinary' Canadians, especially those whose roots in a traditional rural economy have historically insulated them from technological change.

Salt Cod
National Film Board of Canada
Location Manager

Codfish lured the first men across the sea to Canada in the sixteenth century. As SALT COD depicts, catching and processing cod remains an integral part of many a Newfoundlander's life and livelihood.

1956

Royal Canadian Corps of Signals
National Film Board of Canada/
Department of National Defence
Writer

Communication is the key to today's complex army fighting machine. This film examines the important communication role provided by the men and women of the Royal Canadian Corps of Signals.

1957

Canada's Armed Forces
National Film Board of Canada/
Department of National Defence
Writer

A report of the accomplishments on land, sea and air which made 1957 a banner year for the Canadian Army, Navy and Air Force.

Wildlife of the Rocky Mountains
National Film Board of Canada
Commentary

A close-up look at Banff and Jasper—vast zoological gardens of deer, moose, bear, bighorn sheep, birds and small animals, surrounded by snowy peaks.

1958

Canadian Infantrymen
National Film Board of Canada/
Department of National Defence
Writer

An historical look at the infantry soldier. It includes portrayals of the individual, team spirit, training, weapons and actual infantry tactics from World War II.

A Matter Of Survival
**National Film Board of Canada/
Department of National Defence
Writer**

An intimate study of one company's struggle with the need to automate. On one side of the issue is economic reality; on the other, automation's impact on working people.

Sight Unseen
**National Film Board of Canada/
Department of National Defence
Director/Writer**

Produced for the Royal Canadian Navy, this training film schools air crews in the procedures for the Julie Explosive Echo Range System of sonobuoys used in anti-submarine operations.

Survival Series
INTRODUCTION: A PATTERN
FOR STAYING ALIVE
STAY ALIVE IN THE
    SUMMER ARCTIC
STAY ALIVE IN THE WINTER BUSH
STAY ALIVE IN THE WINTER
ARCTIC
**National Film Board of Canada/
Department of National Defence
Writer**

You're stranded in a remote corner of Canada's north. What do you do—and not do—to survive? That question is answered in this series of four training films produced for the Department of National Defence.

Setting Fires For Science
**National Film Board of Canada
Director/Writer**

Down the deserted streets of Autsville, Ontario, a town evacuated for flooding by the St. Lawrence Seaway, building after building is set alight as scientists from Canada's National Research Council learn how to fight fire with fire.
Abridged version: FIRE DETECTIVES

St. Lawrence Burns No. 1–8
**National Film Board of Canada/
National Research Council
Director**

Eight silent films of the burning of houses along the St. Lawrence River as part of scientific research by the National Research Council.

Winter Construction? It Can Be Done
**National Film Board of Canada
Director/Writer**

Revolutionary pre-heating techniques for concrete building materials, special ground preparation and ingenious sheltering devices prove Canada's frigid winters need no longer be the builder's bugbear.

1959

A Day in the Life of Jonathan Mole
National Film Board of Canada
Director/Writer

Bitter and biased, Jonathan Mole dreams of the courtroom trial of an Indian, a Jew and an immigrant in 'Adanac', a land that restricts better jobs to people of 'pure' stock. Despite reasonable arguments, prejudice prevails in this no-holds-barred exposition.

Blessing of the Fishing Fleet at Caraquet, New Brunswick
National Film Board of Canada
Location Manager

Acadian descendents from across North America flocked to Caraquet, New Brunswick in the summer of 1955 for a colourful and historic one-day bicentennial celebration.

1961

Everybody's Prejudiced
National Film Board of Canada
Director/Writer

Is rejecting eggs because they once made you sick the same as hating a new neighbour for no reason at all? The role 'fact' plays in different types of prejudice is opened for discussion in this thoughtful film.

1962

Canada At War
PART 1: DUSK
PART 2: BLITZKRIEG
PART 3: YEAR OF SIEGE
PART 4: DAYS OF INFAMY
PART 5: EBBTIDE
PART 6: TURN OF THE TIDE
PART 7: ROAD TO ORTONA
PART 8: NEW DIRECTIONS
PART 9: THE NORMAN SUMMER
PART 10: CINDERELLA ON THE LEFT
PART 11: CRISIS ON THE HILL
PART 12: V WAS FOR VICTORY
PART 13: THE CLOUDED DAWN
National Film Board of Canada
Director/Writer

The largest documentary effort ever undertaken by the NFB, these 13 half-hour films use historic footage to present World War II from a uniquely Canadian perspective.

Willie Catches On
National Film Board of Canada
Writer

WILLIE CATCHES ON is a realistic attempt to answer the question, how are the seeds of prejudice sown? Although never overt, adult behaviour influences Willie's attitude towards others to the extent that he unquestioningly adjusts to his 'two-faced' world.

1964

Bethune
National Film Board of Canada
Co-Producer/Writer

With incredible perseverance, Canadian-born Norman Bethune devoted his life to the sick and injured. Doctor, humanitarian, thinker and philosopher, his concern for the suffering of others took him wherever he felt the need was greatest.

The Changing City
National Film Board of Canada
Writer

For town planners, civic organizations and the public, the National Housing Act provides the blueprint for federal government resources to meet the housing needs of a growing Canada.

Fields Of Sacrifice
National Film Board of Canada
Director/Producer/Writer

A tribute to the more than one hundred thousand Canadians who have died abroad in the service of their country, FIELDS OF SACRIFICE visits battlefields around the world to help those at home remember.

Return Reservation
National Film Board of Canada
Director/Writer

Discover why Toronto, Canada's most international city, has non-permanent residents to thank for at least part of its metropolitan flavour.

Summerhill
National Film Board of Canada
Director/Producer/Writer

Welcome to Summerhill, a co-educational English boarding school where students are their own masters under the philosophy of founder Alexander Neill, who believes schools should put preparation for life ahead of learning.

1965

Buster Keaton Rides Again
National Film Board of Canada
Writer

BUSTER KEATON RIDES AGAIN is a film about making a film—more precisely, a film that provides an informal study of the famous silent screen star during the production of THE RAILRODDER.

Memorandum
National Film Board of Canada
Co-Director/Writer

It is 20 years after the liberation of prisoners from the wartime death camps. Through a man who remembers, MEMORANDUM poses the question: How much has already been forgotten?

71

Ladies and Gentlemen...
Mr. Leonard Cohen
National Film Board of Canada
Co-Director/Writer

This portrait of a poet follows the 30-year-old Cohen as he comes home to Montreal to "renew his neurotic affiliations." On stage, in the bath or in his three-dollar-a-night hotel room, Cohen's poetic sensibilities are never far from the surface.

Stravinsky
National Film Board of Canada
Writer

An informal study of the great but extremely human dean of modern composers, a man past 80, full of the joy of life, with a long and alert memory for people and events in music.

A Trip Down
Memory Lane
National Film Board of Canada
Producer

Archival movie sequences collide with borrowed commentary to create a bizarre, ironic, yet strangely fitting time-capsule of the twentieth century.

1966
Helicopter Canada
National Film Board of Canada
Writer

It's Canada as you've never seen it before...a spectacular bird's eye view that is at once funny, loving and irreverent.

Never A Backward Step
National Film Board of Canada
Co-Director/Writer

Born in Toronto in 1894, Roy Thomson stepped forward to become Lord Thomson, England's brash Canadian financier with operations on an international scale. His story echoes the lives of many in our money-minded age.

What On Earth!
National Film Board of Canada
Writer

Martians visit and find the prevailing and intelligent form of life on earth to be—no, not humans—automobiles! Delightfully animated and amazingly plausible, WHAT ON EARTH! drives home the prospect of machines overtaking man.

1967
Labyrinth
National Film Board of Canada
Co-Writer

Described as the biggest event in the history of Canadian movies, LABYRINTH was the most popular film at Expo '86. In it, the ancient tradition of man as hero is translated into a compelling and contemporary experience.

To Be Young
Canadian Pacific Railway/Cominco
Writer

Produced for Expo '67, TO BE YOUNG takes the viewer on a journey from birth to adulthood through the collective experiences of the 50 youngsters, 340 teenagers and 65 adults—all non-professional actors—who make up the cast.

Juggernaut
National Film Board of Canada
Writer

To India, where human energy is still the most common source of power comes a Canadian-built atomic reactor. The camera traces this new juggernaut as it makes its six-hundred-mile trek to Rajasthan where it will generate electric power for an entire area.
Abridged version:
ATOMIC JUGGERNAUT

1968
Saul Alinsky Went to War
National Film Board of Canada
Co-Director/Writer

Controversial professional organizer Saul Alinsky wages a war against conditions that keep the poor in poverty by showing blacks in the United States how to find effective, non-violent ways to fight for their rights.

1970
Tiger Child
Kiichi Ichikawa
Director/Writer

The first IMAX film, created for Expo '70 in Osaka, Japan, TIGER CHILD is a poetic work on the agony and brutality of humanity, a travelogue of the human soul.

World of Enrico Fermi
Visual Education Centre
Writer

A biography of a distinguised physicist and a capsule record of a most dynamic period in the history of physics.

1971
The Apprentice
Potterton Productions
Producer

Delinquency and relationships are examined in this story of a Montreal youth who becomes involved with two young women and a crime before his eventual death.

Death of a Legend
National Film Board of Canada
Narrator

Humanity's lack of sensitivity and appreciation for the wolf is an indication of how we treat the natural world and what we are doing to it through ignorance.

The Noblest of Callings...The Vilest of Trades

Canadian Broadcasting Corporation
Co-Director/Writer

Former prime ministers John Diefenbaker and Lester Pearson comment on the role of the back-bencher in this exploration of the effectiveness of the parliamentary process in Canada, the United Kingdom and the United States.

1972

The One Man Band that Went to Wall Street

Potterton Productions
Writer

An animated film explaining in a simple and entertaining way the workings of the New York Stock Exchange.

The People's Railway

Potterton Productions
Producer/Writer

A cinema verite look at the Canadian National Railway through the activities and personalities of some of its employees.

1973

Catskinner Keen

National Film Board of Canada
Director/Producer/Writer

R.J. 'Catskinner' Keen of Edmonton represents a new breed of western businessman. Equally at home around a board-room table or a campfire, his quiet, hard-working determination makes him a millionaire in the best western tradition.

Cavendish Country

National Film Board of Canada
Director/Producer/Writer

Singer, pilot, night security guard, Cal Cavendish of Calgary is one of Canada's finest songwriters. The camera follows Cavendish as he strives to make it big in country-western music while keeping his integrity intact.

Grierson

National Film Board of Canada
Writer

Known as the father of documentary film, John Grierson's early commitment to filmmaking in the public service became a model for many. Some of those filmmakers most influenced share their insights into the contributions of this film pioneer.

Starblanket
National Film Board of Canada
Director/Producer/Writer

At 26, Noel Starblanket is one of North America's youngest Indian Chiefs. Having taken his great-grandfather's advice to "learn the wit and cunning of the white man," he is shown to be one of its most effective leaders as well.

1974
Dreamland: A History of Early Canadian Movies 1895–1939
Great Canadian Moving Picture Co./ National Film Board of Canada
Director/Writer

DREAMLAND is a history of early Canadian movies from 1895 to 1939. Irreverent, nostalgic, engaging and rich in anecdotes, it presents precious surviving film footage from an innocent era.

King of the Hill
National Film Board of Canada
Co-Director/Writer

Footage shot over the 1972 and 1973 baseball seasons provides an insider's view of an 'average' year for Ferguson Jenkins, one of the few Canadian-born baseball players to star in the major leagues.

The Players
National Film Board of Canada/ South Australian Film Corporation
Director/Writer

The Stratford Players are famous for making Shakespeare popular in Canada. So what are they doing—and what was it like—performing Moliere in Australia? This enlightening on-stage and behind-the-scenes tour tells all.

Stress: The Two-faced Enemy
Informedia
Co-Producer/Co-Director/Co-Writer

Meet Dr. Hans Selye of the University of Montreal, whose revolutionary theory suggests that stress is an alarm reaction to disease, injury or mental pressure. Since the reaction is through the pituitary and adrenal glands, he hypothesizes that hormone treatment may combat disease.

Thunderbirds in China
National Film Board of Canada
Co-Producer/Writer

The University of British Columbia's Thunderbirds hockey team was the first foreign team to be invited to the People's Republic. Through their experience, we gain insight into China, ourselves and Canada's national sport.

Van's Camp
National Film Board of Canada
Co-Director/Producer/Writer

Americans pay big bucks to land trophy-size freshwater fish at Van Bliss's Lac La Ronge Saskatchewan camp. But all is not always well in paradise. As Bliss puts it, "fish are not a problem, but people can be."

1975

Arctic IV
National Film Board of Canada
Writer

Under at least six feet of ice and in the most extreme conditions, undersea explorers probe the mysteries of polar waters. A film of discovery, ARCTIC IV examines the consequences of understanding and exploiting Canada's top of the world.

His Worship, Mr. Montreal
National Film Board of Canada
Co-Director/Co-Producer/Writer

Charismatic. Convict. Consummate Politician. Camillien Houde, the mayor of Montreal was all that and more. A combination of archival footage and interviews provides an intimate portrait of a bombastic man, his city and his times.

Los Canadienses
National Film Board of Canada
Narrator

LOS CANADIENSES is the dynamic story of the twelve hundred Canadian volunteers who joined the Mackenzie-Papineau Battalion to fight in the Spanish Civil War of 1936-39.

Scoggie
National Film Board of Canada
Commentary

Anchored by a childhood memory and committed to the sea, his sailboat, his freedom and the few friends who have remained in this economically depressed area, Scoggie Watson is determined to continue living by Lac Bras d'Or.

The Summer Before
Crawley Films
Director/Writer

The finish line is the 1976 Olympic Games and athletes across Canada are preparing themselves to compete among the world's best.

Whistling Smith
National Film Board of Canada
Writer

The camera walks the beat with Sgt. Bernie 'Whistling' Smith in Vancouver's colourful east-side. One of a series of seven PACIFICANADA films, it is a telling look at the underbelly of big city life.

1976

The Land: A New Priority
National Film Board of Canada
Narration

Rural communities in Senegal, Kenya, Mauritius, Pakistan and Sri Lanka serve as deceptively lush backdrops in this documentary about the struggles of rural people in the third world.

The Sword Of The Lord
National Film Board of Canada
Writer

An examination of the drive, determination and—most of all—faith that brought 22-year-old Jim Hunter, a member of Canada's national ski team, to the brink of international success.

Volcano: An Inquiry Into The Life And Death Of Malcolm Lowry
National Film Board of Canada
Co-Director/Co-Producer/Writer

UNDER THE VOLCANO is considered by some to be the novel of the century. Its author, Malcolm Lowry, elicits a no-less passionate response. This is a biographical tour of a man who took 14 years to write a classic, then drank himself into the grave.

1977

Henry Ford's America
National Film Board of Canada
Director/Producer/Writer

Henry Ford I gave us the Model T, which gave us mobility, automation, organized labour, exhaust fumes, the consumer movement and Henry Ford II. As the film points out, it was only a car, but it changed the course of history.

The Vacant Lot
National Film Board of Canada
Producer/Writer

Land owned by the Montreal Jewish General Hospital was idle, and so were many of the seniors living nearby. Enter one newly retired Mr. Aaron, whose vision of turning aimless land into a garden brought both fiscal and personal gains.

The Champions
1978 – Part 1 & 2
Part 1: Unlikely Warriors
Part 2: Trappings Of Power
National Film Board of Canada/ Canadian Broadcasting Corporation
Director/Producer/Writer

1986 – Part 3
Part 3: The Final Battle
Director/Writer

Brittain's acclaimed political trilogy is an examination of the careers of Pierre Elliott Trudeau and René Lévesque from 1967 to 1985. Meticulously researched, it is a fascinating portrait of Canada's most notable political warriors.

1978

The Dionne Quintuplets
**National Film Board of Canada/
Canadian Broadcasting Corporation
Director/Producer**

Born in a log farmhouse, taken from
their family and prized as exhibits, the
story of the Dionne quintuplets is one
of miraculous survival. The film
presents the stranger-than-fiction
reality of the sisters' first 21 years.

Has Anybody Here
Seen Canada?
**National Film Board of Canada/
Canadian Broadcasting Corporation**
in co-operation with **Great Canadian
Moving Picture Co.
Writer**

It started with the establishment of
the National Film Board in 1939. By
1941, Canada's first Academy Award
was in hand. This documentary traces
the history of Canadian filmmaking
from 1939 to 1953, and poses its own
questions about the future.

In Search of
Bermuda Pirates
**Alan Landsburg Productions Inc.
Director/Co-producer/Writer**

A pleasure cruise off the Florida coast
becomes a nightmare as modern-day
pirates terrorize boaters.

In Search of the
Great Lakes Triangle
**Alan Landsburg Productions Inc.
Director/Co-producer/Writer**

Considered among the most beautiful
waterways in the world, the Great
Lakes hold hidden perils for the
unsuspecting boater. Are the wrecks
merely tragic coincidence, or is
something else at work?

Secrets of the
Bermuda Triangle
**Alan Landsburg Productions Inc.
Director/Co-producer/Writer**

Dramatized account of some of
the true, startling cases of total
disappearance of vessels, airplanes
and humans from the Bermuda
Triangle in its long and heady
history as a mysterious graveyard.

Small is Beautiful:
Impressions of
Fritz Schumacher
**National Film Board of Canada
Director/Writer**

A look at economist Ernst Friedrich
Schumacher whose book SMALL IS
BEAUTIFUL: A STUDY OF ECONOMICS
AS IF PEOPLE MATTERED established
him as a gentle revolutionary who
puts people before product.

1979

Bow and Arrow
National Film Board of Canada
Writer

One of the first tools known in which energy could be stored and released at will, the bow and arrow has a special place in world history and an enduring fascination in modern times.

Marooned in the Land God Gave Cain
Rosebud Films
Narrator

In 1542, Marguerite de Roberval and her lover were marooned on a deserted island by her angry uncle. Despite the death of her companion and their baby, Marguerite survived until Basque fishermen rescued her two years later.

Paperland: The Bureaucrat Observed
National Film Board of Canada/ Canadian Broadcasting Corporation
Director/Writer

Whether in Canada, Hungary, the Vatican or the Virgin Islands, the bureaucrat shapes our lives from the cradle to the grave. In PAPERLAND we, the people, and they, the bureaucrats, share in one common feeling— complete helplessness.

The Spirit of the River to China
Rosebud Films
Narrator

An arduous canoe trip is the stage for this probe into the explosive relationship between Etienne Brule, the first European to live among Indians, and Jesuit priest Father Jean de Brebeuf, whose mission was to convert Natives.

1980

The Inheritance
National Film Board of Canada
Narration

The Quebec Referendum forces two sons, one a liberal businessman and one a former minister of labour in the Parti Québécois government, to make a painful choice between Quebec and Canada.

The Lost Pharaoh: The Search for Akhenaten
National Film Board of Canada
Canadian Broadcasting Corporation
Director

Canadian archaeologist Dr. Donald Redford painstakingly sifts the sands in search of the tomb of Akhenaten, an enigmatic ruler from 1375 to 1358 B.C., whose religious beliefs turned Egypt on its ear.

Wop May
Marmalade Animation
Writer

Animated short on the courage and selflessness of pioneer aviator Wop May.

1981

Bamboo, Lions and Dragons
National Film Board of Canada
Writer
Vancouver's Chinatown is the setting for this probe of the experiences of two Chinese families—one headed by a 93-year-old immigrant, the other second generation suburbanites—who have come to call Canada home.

Future Ground
Stonehaven Productions
Narrator

For the air-carrier industry new technologies impose changes both on the ground and in the air.

On Guard For Thee
PART I: THE MOST DANGEROUS SPY
PART 2: BLANKET OF ICE
PART 3: SHADOWS OF A HORSEMAN
National Film Board of Canada/
Canadian Broadcasting Corporation
Director/Co-Producer/Writer

Canada's national security operations are laid bare in this three-part series of films which encompasses events ranging from the Gouzenko spy affair in 1946 to the 1981 creation of a civilian security service.

Running Man
Canadian Broadcasting Corporation
Director

Televised as part of the CBC series "For the Record," RUNNING MAN is the dramatic story of a married high school teacher and father of two as he comes to terms with his homosexuality.

1982

An Honourable Member
Canadian Broadcasting Corporation
Director

A woman cabinet minister provides an insider's glimpse into the world of protocol, bureaucracy and back room deals in this drama produced for the CBC series "For the Record."

Dream Horse
Canadian Broadcasting Corporation
Director/Producer/Writer

Mort and Marjoh Levy's dream of owning a champion thoroughbred racehorse falls apart as their winning two-year-old, Deputy Minister, fails to live up to expectations.

1983

The Accident
Canadian Broadcasting Corporation
Director

The aftermath of tragedy is the subject of this examination of the lives of three families, each of which lost a child when the roof of a hockey arena collapsed.

Something to Celebrate
**National Film Board of Canada/
Canadian Broadcasting Corporation
Director/Producer/Writer**

The seniors showcased in this film are
anything but stereotypical. All at
least 70, they pursue careers, hobbies,
friendships—the simple pleasures of
living—with a zest that keeps them
young at heart.

The Children's Crusade
**National Film Board of Canada/
Canadian Broadcasting Corporation
Director/Producer/Writer**

An examination of the scandal surrounding the American Peace Corps-
inspired Company of Young
Canadians, the 'power to the people'
decade of the 1960s that spawned it,
and the surprisingly positive legacy it
left behind.

1984
The First Canadian
Astronaut
**Filmcentres Productions Inc.
Narrator**

A documentary on the first Canadian
astronaut, Marc Garneau, from the
competition which found him to the
final shuttle countdown in 1984.

Act of God – A
Gathering in Denendeh
**Gary Nichols and Associates Ltd.
Writer**

Anticipation turns to disappointment when a quirk of nature
prevents Pope John Paul II from
reaching Fort Simpson, Northwest
Territories, where members of the
scattered Dene Nation have
gathered to hear the pontiff.

Overtime
**National Film Board of Canada
Writer**

Long after other middle-aged men
have settled into arm-chair sports
enthusiasm, they're still playing hard.
They are the Toronto Lakeshore Old-
timers, a team of hockey players
whose passion is as strong as ever,
even if their bodies are not.

1985
Canada's Sweetheart:
The Saga of Hal C. Banks
**National Film Board of Canada/
Canadian Broadcasting Corporation
Director/Producer/Writer**

Recruited at the request of the
Canadian Government, Harold
Banks brutally obliterated the
Communist-led Canadian Seamen's
union and blacklisted thousands of
seamen in a reign of terror and
intimidation.

Earthwatch
Les Productions Prisma Inc.
Director/Producer/Writer

Produced using the avant-garde Showscan technique, EARTHWATCH is a highly impressionistic documentary of how Canada's seemingly insurmountable transportation and communication barriers were conquered in the quest to build the nation.

First Stop, China
National Film Board of Canada
Writer

When Les Grands Ballets Canadiens went on tour in the Far East, their schedule of 40 performances in 20 weeks in 10 cities gave new meaning to the adage "the show must go on." Despite a litany of obstacles, East met West with well-earned applause.

1986

Long Lance
National Film Board of Canada
Writer

Sylvester Clark Long was half Indian, half white, but in North Carolina he was considered black. Looking for his real roots, he took the name Chief Buffalo Child Long Lance and set out on a life of deception, fame and tragedy.

Mobility
National Film Board of Canada
Writer/Narrator

Mobility takes us to cities in Africa, India, Asia and South America where vast influxes of people are placing great demands on all forms of transit systems; where the middle-class and the poor clash over the road out of poverty.

Tommy Douglas: Keeper of the Flame
National Film Board of Canada
Writer

From champion boxer to fiery preacher to leader of the federal New Democratic Party, Tommy Douglas was a man whose vision of social justice was the catalyst for 'radical' reforms—including Canada's medicare system.

1987

No Accident
National Film Board of Canada
Narrator

A plea for not mixing drinking and driving, as Bert Robertson tells how his eight-year-old son was killed in the family driveway by a drunk driver.

Those Roos Boys and Friends

Film Arts/Pineapple Productions
Narrator

Len and Charlie Roos, from Gault, Ontario, were adventurers, promoters and pioneers in cinema and sound technology. They made the first Canadian feature film during World War I.

1988

The King Chronicle

PART 1: MACKENZIE KING AND THE UNSEEN HAND
PART 2: MACKENZIE KING AND THE GREAT BEYOND
PART 3: MACKENZIE KING AND THE ZOMBIE ARMY
National Film Board of Canada/ Canadian Broadcasting Corporation
Director/Writer/Narrator

Described as an "ugly toad", the Great Conciliator, William Lyon Mackenzie King was the most successful politician in Canadian history. In Donald Brittain's three-part saga, King is portrayed as a mass of contradictions, the dark side of Canadians.

See No Evil

National Film Board of Canada
Narrator

Challenging the system: Stan Grey's fight against health hazards in the workplace.

1989

Goddess Remembered

National Film Board of Canada
Co-writer

The spiritual journey of Earth's people began with the idea of a goddess, the Great Mother who linked humans with the world around them.

1991

Family: A Loving Look at CBC Radio

National Film Board of Canada
Writer/Director
Completed by Robert Duncan

An intriguing behind-the-scenes look at the unique cast of characters who make up Canada's cost-to-coast radio 'family'.

Films On Brittain

1989

Brittain on Brittain
Access and National Film Board of Canada
Ray Harper, Producer

An engaging thirteen part video series celebrating the best of Donald Brittain. Each episode features colourful interviews with Brittain interwoven with more than a dozen of his finest films.

1991

Brittain Directs
Kent Martin and Adam Symansky, National Film Board of Canada

A behind-the-scenes investigation of Brittain in action to be completed in 1991.

Films Also Attributed To Donald Brittain

1956

Fishing With Ketch
Carling Brewers
Writer

1957

The Silver Chain
Canadian Broadcasting Corporation
Writer

1958

Dot
Canadian Broadcasting Corporation
Writer

1959

The Royal Canadian Mind
Canadian Broadcasting Corporation
Writer

1964

Mosca
Canadian Broadcasting Corporation
Director/Producer/Writer

The Campaigners
Canadian Broadcasting Corporation
Director/Producer/Writer

1967

The Granby Election
Canadian Broadcasting Corporation
Director/Writer

Film Awards

Film Awards

Arctic IV
Special Mention
25th International Festival of
Mountain & Exploration Films
Trento, Italy
May 22–28, 1977

Bethune
Diploma
19th International Film Festival
Edinburgh, Scotland
August, 1965

First Prize
4th International Documentary and
Short Film Festival
Leipzig, Germany
November, 1965

Diploma of Merit
Short Film Competition
Melbourne Film Festival
Melbourne, Australia
June, 1966

Gold Medal
International Red Cross and Health
Film Festival
Sofia, Bulgaria
1967

Bow and Arrow
Red Ribbon Award—
Sports and Leisure Category
24th Annual American Film Festival
New York, USA
June 14–19, 1982

Buster Keaton Rides Again
First Prize (ex-aequo),
Medium Length Films
Festival of Canadian Films
Montreal International Film Festival
Montreal, Canada
March, 1966

Silver Trophy—
Documentary Category
Tenth San Francisco International
Film Festival
San Francisco, USA
March, 1966

Special Prize—CIDALC
XVII International Exhibition
of the Documentary Film
Venice, Italy
March, 1966

Best General Information Film
Canadian Film Awards
Montreal, Canada
1966

Special Prize for Best Biographical
Documentary
Melbourne International
Film Festival
Melbourne, Australia
1967

First Prize—Music, Literature
and Films Category
American Film Festival
New York, USA
June, 1967

Gold Medal MIFED
(Milan Film Market)
International Contest
of Public Relations
Milan, Italy
October 18, 1968

Canada's Sweetheart: The Saga of Hal C. Banks

Nellie—Best Television Director
Actra Awards
Toronto, Canada
April 2, 1986

Anik Award—Best Drama
(tied with Charlie Grant's War)
CBC
Ottawa, Canada
May 14, 1986

Gemini Award—Best Direction
in a Dramatic Program

Gemini Award—Best Original
Screenplay (Donald Brittain and
Richard Nielsen)

Gemini Awards
Toronto, Canada
December 3–4, 1986

Catskinner Keen

Award for Best
Location Documentary
Festival of World Television
Hollywood, USA
October 1, 1974

The Champions

Part I
Etrog—Best Documentary
60 minutes and over
Etrog—Best Non-Dramatic Script
Canadian Film Awards
Toronto, Canada
September 14–21, 1978

Part III
Best Documentary Award—
Social-Political Category
Banff Television Festival
Banff, Canada
June 7–13, 1987

Gemini Award—Best Documentary

Gemini Award—Best Direction
in a Documentary,
Gemini Awards,
Presenting Body
Toronto, Canada
December 8–9, 1987

The Changing City

Chris Certificate Award—
Information Category
12th Annual Columbus
Film Festival
Columbus, Ohio, USA
1964–65

Honourable Mention
Third International Film Contest
27th Congress on Housing
and Planning
Jerusalem, Israel
June 21–28, 1964

The Dionne Quintuplets
Chris Bronze Plaque Award—
Social Studies Category
27th Annual Film Festival for the
Film Council of Greater Columbus
Columbus, Ohio, U.S.A
November 25, 1979

Second Prize—Social
and Political Category
International Festival of Films for TV
Banff, Canada
August 23–September 1, 1979

Dreamland
Etrog—Best Non-Dramatic Script
Canadian Film Awards
Niagara-on-the-Lake, Ontario
October 7–12, 1975

Everybody's Prejudiced
Chris Certificate Award—
Mental Health Category
10th Annual Columbus
Film Festival
Columbus, Ohio, USA
September 28, 1962

Fields of Sacrifice
Chris Certificate Award—
Information-Education Category
12th Annual Columbus
Film Festival
Columbus, Ohio, U.S.A
September, 1964

Certificate of Merit—
General Information Category
Canadian Film Awards
Toronto, Canada
May 8, 1964

Second Prize
Victoria International Film Festival
Victoria, Canada
July 1–August 15, 1964

Grierson
Diploma of Merit
23rd Film Festival
Melbourne, Australia
June, 1974

Robert Flaherty Award
Society of Film & Television Arts
London, England
March, 1974

Best Profile Documentary
9th Festival of World Television
Hollywood, USA
September 30, 1973

Bronze Reel Award:
Third Best Film—Over All Winner,
Personality Category
17th International Film Festival
San Francisco, USA
October 17–28, 1973

Etrog—Best Documentary
Canadian Film Awards
Montreal, Canada
October 8–12, 1973

Helicopter Canada

Canuck Award—First Prize
Canadian Travel Film Awards
Toronto, Canada
1967–68

Best General Information Film
(ex aequo)
Canadian Film Awards
.Toronto, Ontario
1967–68

Special Prize: "For providing
a superbly appropriate and
inspiring opportunity for
Canadians to view their country
in the Centennial Year"
Canadian Film Awards
Toronto, Canada
1967–68

Henry Ford's America

Best Non-Fiction Television Film
5th Annual International Emmy
Awards
New York, USA
November 21, 1977

Bronze Medallion—Documentary
Over 27 Minutes Category
HemisFilm 78, International
Film Festival
San Antonio, Texas, USA
February 6–8, 1978

Certificate of Merit
13th International Film Festival
Chicago, USA
November 4–17, 1977

Chris Bronze Plaque—
Social Studies Category
26th International Film Festival
Columbus, Ohio, USA
October 19, 1978

Etrog—Best Non-Dramatic Script
Canadian Film Awards
Toronto, Canada
November 20, 1977

Honorable Mention
APGA Film Festival
Washington, USA
March 19–23, 1978

Red Ribbon Award—
Features, History and
Economics Category
20th Annual American Festival
New York, USA
May 21–26, 1978

Silver Screen Award For
Outstanding Creativity in
the Production of Audio-visual
Communications in International
Competition
Industrial Film Festival
Bellwood, USA
April 27, 1978

Special Jury Award for
Outstanding Achievement—
Film as Communication Competition
21st Annual International
Film Festival
San Francisco, USA
October 5–16, 1977

89

The King Chronicle

Chris Statuette Award—
Social Studies Category
36th Annual International
Film Festival
Columbus, Ohio, USA
October 26–28, 1988

King of the Hill

Main Prize
Sport Film Festival
Oberhausen, West Germany
October, 1975

Long Lance

Award for Best Script—
Non-Fiction Category
13th Annual Alberta Film
and Television Awards Festival
Edmonton, Canada
March 21, 1987

Memorandum

Special Mention—
Medium Length Films
Festival of Canadian Films
Montreal International Film Festival
Montreal, Canada
August, 1966

Golden Gate Award:
First Prize, Essay Category
10th San Francisco
International Film Festival
San Francisco, USA
March, 1966

Certificate of Merit—
Television Films Category
9th Vancouver International
Film Festival
Vancouver, Canada
October, 1966

Lion of St. Marc: First Prize
XVII Exhibition of the
Documentary Film
Venice, Italy
August/September, 1966

Never a Backward Step

Redwood Award for Special Merit in
the Film-as-Communication Section
San Francisco Film Festival
San Francisco, U.S.A
March, 1968

Notable Film Award
Calvin Workshop Awards
New York, USA
September, 1968

Blue Ribbon Award: First Prize—
Biography and History Category
10th American Film Festival
New York, USA
June 1, 1968

Best Documentary over 30 minutes
Canadian Film Awards
Toronto, Ontario
October 4, 1968

Paperland: The Bureaucrat Observed

Genie Award—
Outstanding Documentary
30 minutes and over

Genie Award—
Outstanding Direction
in a Documentary

Genie Award—
Outstanding Editing
in a Documentary,
to Richard Todd

Genie Award—
Outstanding non-dramatic script,
to Donald Brittain, Ron Blumer and
John T. Random
March 19, 1980

The People's Railway

Silver Hugo—
Business and Industrial Category
Chicago International Film Festival
November 8–17, 1974

See No Evil

Merit Award—Narration
8th Atlantic Film and Video Festival
Halifax, Canada
October 26–28, 1988

Something to Celebrate

Honourable Mention
B'nai B'rith Awards
Toronto, Canada
November 26, 1984

The President's Chris Award
for Best of Festival Production
32nd International Film Festival
Columbus, Ohio, USA
November 3, 1984

Stravinsky

Special Mention—Short Film Category
Festival of Canadian Films
Montreal International Film Festival
Montreal, Canada
August 1965

Award in TV—Information Category
Canadian Film Awards
Montreal, Canada
1966

Tommy Douglas: Keeper of the Flame

Gemini Award—Best Writing in a
Documentary Program or Series
Gemini Awards
Toronto, Canada
December 8–9, 1987

A Trip Down Memory Lane

Certificate of Motion Picture Excellence
10th San Francisco International
Film Festival
San Francisco, USA
1966–1967

Plaque of the Lion of St. Marc—
Teledocumentary Category
17th Exhibition of the
Documentary Film
Venice, Italy

Volcano: An Inquiry into the Life and Death of Malcolm Lowry

Asolo Award
International Festival of Films
on Art and Artists
Asolo, Italy
May 26–31, 1979

Actra Award—Best Writer,
Visual Medium
ACTRA Annual Awards
Montreal, Canada
March 23, 1977

Blue Ribbon Award—
Feature Length Documentaries
19th Annual American Film Festival
New York, USA
May 23–28, 1977

Etrog—Best Documentary

Etrog—Best Direction,
to Donald Brittain

Etrog—Best non-dramatic script,
to Donald Brittain and John Kramer
Canadian Film Awards
Toronto, Canada
October 18–24, 1976

Grand Prize—Literature
International Leipzig Documentary
and Short Film Festival
Leipzig, West Germany
November, 1976

First Prize—Literature
American Film Awards
New York, USA
June, 1977

Grand Prize
International West German
Short Film Festival
Oberhausen, West Germany
April, 1977

What on Earth!

Silver Seal of the City of Trieste
International Festival
of Science-Fiction Films
Trieste, Italy
1967–1968

Blue Ribbon Award—Animation
13th American Film Festival
New York, USA
May 11–15, 1971

Cup
Festival International
du Film a Format Reduit
Salerno, Italy
October 12–18, 1970

Whistling Smith

Etrog—Best Editing,
to Jean-Pierre Joutel
Canadian Film Awards
Niagara-on-the-Lake, Canada
October 7–12, 1975

Red Ribbon
18th American Film Festival
New York, USA
1976

Honours and Distinctions

Honours and Distinctions

Centennial Medal

"Given to Distinguished Canadians in honour of Canada's 100th Birthday" by the Rt. Hon. Roland Michener, Governor General of Canada
July 1, 1967

John Grierson Award
The Champions

Canadian Film Awards
Toronto, Canada
September 14–21, 1978

National Film Board of Canada: A Retrospective, Part II

Documentary: Donald Brittain, Museum of Modern Art
New York, USA
March 26-May 12, 1981

Toronto City Award For Excellence in Canadian Production

Toronto, Canada
September 5–14, 1985

Ontario Film Institute Award, lifetime achievement award for excellence in Canadian filmmaking

Toronto, Ontario
1986

Honourary Doctor Of Letters, York University

Toronto, Canada
Conferred Spring Convocation, 1987

John Grierson International Gold Medal Award

130th SMPTE Technical Conference
New York, USA
October 15–19, 1988

Margaret Collier Award

"Presented to a writer for a body of work in television—
given posthumously
Academy of Canadian Cinema and Television
Toronto, Canada
December 5, 1989

Appointed Officer to the Order of Canada

Ottawa, Canada
April 30, 1989 (posthumous investiture, April 18, 1990)

Bibliography

Bibliography

Arsenault, Andre-guy. "Shooting Brittain's King." *Cinema Canada* 142 (June 1987): pp. 8–9.

Base, Ron. "A journey through hell with a madman." *Maclean's* 89.6 (April 5, 1976): p. 69.

"Battles of Brittain, The." *Globe and Mail* (Toronto) – Metro Edition (September 6, 1986): pp. C1,C3.

Bemrose, John. "The Champions, Part III: The Final Battle." *Maclean's* (September 15, 1985): p. 56.

Blumer, Ron. "Donald Brittain's Volcano." *Cinema Canada* 3.28 (May 1976): pp. 47–48.

Blumer, Ronald. *The films of Donald Brittain: the first 20 years.* Montreal: National Film Board of Canada, 1979.

Blumer, Ronald and Susan Schouten. "Green stripe and common sense." *Cinema Canada* 15 (August/September 1974): pp. 36–40.

"Brittain awarded Grierson Medal." *Globe and Mail* (Toronto) – Metro Edition (October 5, 1988): p. C8.

"The Champions, part 3: The Final Battle." *Variety* 324 (September 3, 1986): p. 22.

Coulombe, Michel and Marcel Jean. *Le dictionnaire du cinema quebecois.* Montreal: Boreal, 1988. Pp. 65–66.

"Donald Brittain: A Tribute." *Content* (November/December 1989): pp. 28–29.

Dorland, Michael. "Rule Brittania: the filmmaking saga of Don C. Brittain." *Cinema Canada* 126 (January 1986): pp. 11–20.

Duncan, Robert. "Donald Brittain remembered." *Actrascope* V.17 #2 (Fall 1989): pp. 27–28.

"Earthwatch: a film on Canada in the magic of Showscan." *Performing Arts in Canada* 22. (Winter 1985): p. 87.

Friesen, Ralph. "The King Chronicle." *Cinema Canada* 152 (May 1988): p. 26.

Groen Rick. "A Day with Donald Brittain." *Globe and Mail* (Toronto) – Metro Edition (July 24, 1989): p. C7.

"Henry Ford's America." *Wilson Library Bulletin* 52. (June 1978): p. 805.

Hicks, Wessely. "Brittain takes a crack at drama while New York shows his works." *TV Times* (*The Montreal Gazette*) (February 14 to February 20, 1981): p. 11.

Ibranyi-kiss, A. "Dreamland." *Cinema Canada* 16 (October/November 1974): pp. 54–57.

Johnson, Brian D. "A chronicler for a nation." *Maclean's* 101.14 (March 28, 1988): pp. 42–45.

Johnson, Bryan. "Brittain's winning the battle—people know his films if not his name." *Globe and Mail* (March 27, 1976): p. 27.

Kaplan, W. "Canada's Sweetheart: The Saga of Hal C. Banks – Brittain D." *Historical Journal of Film Radio and Television* (1987): V7, N1, pp. 77–81.

Knelman, Martin. "For King and country." *Saturday Night* 103.4 (April 1988): pp. 65–66.

Lanken, Dane. "The documentary— what TV can do best?" *Broadcaster* (January 1978): pp. 6–9.

Levine, Holly. "NFB remembers." *Motion* 5.1 (January 1976): pp. 11–12.

Lewis, Robert. "New light in some dark corners." *Maclean's* 94.44 (November 2, 1981): p. 28.

McCormick, Marion. "Donald Brittain's precious legacy is national treasure." *Montreal Gazette* (July 24, 1989).

Milne, T. "Volcano." *Monthly Film Bulletin* 44.529 (April 1977): p. 83.

Mollins, Carl. "A master of film." *Maclean's* 102.31 (July 31, 1989): p. 40.

Morris, Peter. *The film companion*. Toronto: Irwin, 1984. Pp. 43–44.

Nelson, Joyce. "Canada's Sweetheart: The Saga of Hal C. Banks." *Cinema Canada* 126 (January 1986): pp. 16.

Nolan, Brian. "Donald Brittain: a tribute – will we ever see his like again?" *Content* (November– December 1989): pp. 28–29.

"(Obituary)." *Variety* (weekly) (July 26, 1989).

"(Obituary)." *Variety* (weekly) (August 9, 1989).

Pevere, Geoff. "Canada's Sweetheart: The Saga of Hal C. Banks." *Canadian Forum* 65. (March 1986): p. 39.

Pratley, Gerald. *Torn Sprockets: The Uncertain Project of Canadian Films*. Delaware: University of Delaware Press, 1987.

Alison Reid and Louisa Dupre. *Who's who in Canadian film and television/Qui est qui au cinema et a la television au Canada*. Toronto: Academy of Canadian Cinema and Televison/Academie canadienne du cinema et de la television, 1989. pp. 332–333.

Riches, Hester. "Oscar's in sight: Don Brittain on Lowry's Volcano." *The Peak* (March 25, 1977): p. 9.

Robinson, Brian. "Sweetheart of the lake scum (Hal C. Banks)." *Canadian Dimension* 19. (January-February 1986): p. 41–42.

Thompson, J.H. "The King Chronicle." *Canadian Historical Review* (1988): V69, N4, pp. 503–510.

"Volcano." *Time* 110. (November 7, 1977): pp. 92–93.

Weintraub, William. "A eulogy for Donald Brittain." *Cinema Canada* 166 (September 1989): pp. 4–5.

Wolfe, Morris. "Donald Brittain's fresh view of our epic battle." *Saturday Night* 93.3 (April 1978): pp. 63–64.

"Writing for the screen: six interviews with Canadian writers." *Pot Pourri* (NFB) (Summer 1976): pp. 2–3.

Zanotto, P. "Asolo Film-Festival 1979—Problems of years." *Bn-Bianco E. Nero* (1979): V40, N5–6, pp. 132–136. (In Italian only.)

Zerbisias, Antonia. "An appetite for the sensations of life." *Toronto Star* (July 23, 1989)

Biography

Biography

by Ron Blumer

Cigarette dangling unlit from his mouth, Brittain himself comes on as a character from some 1930's movie; the unkempt sardonic newspaperman with an off-handed sense of humour, a good taste for whisky and a passion for baseball.

Ronald Blumer, critic

He speaks a language all his own, all the more powerful because he yells his innuendoes at you.

Mark Blandford, Montreal *Gazette*

Suddenly Don Brittain is becoming a cult figure, after winning countless prizes at key film festivals around the world and already having captured 16 Canadian film awards since 1963.

Today, this guy whose artistic accomplishments are about to be carved into tablets of stone is off to a poker game with the boys while his wife attends a concert.

Sid Adilman, *Toronto Star*

Donald Brittain was born in Ottawa in 1928. He attended Queen's University, Kingston, and was a police reporter at the Ottawa Journal from 1951 to 1954. He then drifted in Mexico, Europe and Africa. After brief stints as a foreign correspondent in Tangier, and an interpreter in a small brothel on the Cote d'Azur, he ended up broke in the Russian sector of occupied Vienna and shipped back to Canada to begin a film career.

He worked exclusively for the National Film Board of Canada from 1955 to 1968, when he was invited to Japan to create a million-dollar multi-media show—TIGER CHILD—for Expo '70 in Osaka. He then free-lanced, the bulk of his work with the National Film Board. He filmed in 18 countries, on five continents. By 1977 he had contributed 96 films. His work has been exhibited at almost all of the world's major festivals. His awards include the Lion of St. Mark, Venice; the Golden Dove of Peace, Leipzig; the Golden Gate Award, San Francisco; the Blue Ribbon Awards, New York; and five Etrogs at the Canadian Film Awards. His feature VOLCANO was nominated for an Academy Award in 1977. In total three of the films he wrote were nominated for Oscars.

His first wife, Barbara Tuer of Haileybury, died in 1953. He remarried, to Brigitta Halbig of Hamburg, in 1963. He lived in Montreal until his death, with his wife and two children.

Photo Credits

Photo Credits

Front Cover, Title Page

Donald Brittain circa 1975. Photo from the National Film Board of Canada, S-16559.

The Man

Title Page   Donald Brittain circa 1980. Photo by Rick Bujold, NFB.

p.3   Donald Brittain Circa 1975. Photo from the National Film Board of Canada, S-16559.

p.4   Donald Brittain on location, circa 1975. Photo from the National Film Board of Canada, S-16570.

p.6   Brittain on the set of CANADA'S SWEETHEART with Andreas Poulsson, Susan Trow, Claudette Messier and unidentified, 1986. Photo from the National Film Board of Canada.

p.8   Brittain with Producer Adam Symansky. Photo by Ron Diamond, the National Film Board of Canada, 2874-8A9.

p.10   Brittain recording narration at NFB studio. From the collection of Doug Keifer.

p.12   Brittain during the filming of THE KING CHRONICLE, 1988. Photo from the National Film Board of Canada, 3038-13A.

The Filmmaker

Title Page   Donald Brittain filming VOLCANO, 1976. Photo from the National Film Board of Canada, S-15051.

p.14   *Lower left:* Brittain with Sean McCann (King) on the set of THE KING CHRONICLE, 1988. Photo from the National Film Board of Canada, 3066-32A.

Upper right: Adam Symansky, Producer THE CHAMPIONS: THE FINAL BATTLE, 1986. Photo from the National Film Board of Canada, 2874-23A.

p.16   Brittain on location in France for FIELDS OF SACRIFICE, 1964. Photo from the National Film Board of Canada, S-399.

p.19   Brittain, Jean-Pierre Joutel and Julian Olsen editing THE MOST DANGEROUS SPY. Photo from the National Film Board of Canada.

p.20   Brittain with John Spotton at Bergen-Belsen, shooting MEMORANDUM, 1965. Photo from the National Film Board of Canada.

p.22   Brittain with Maury Chaykin (Banks) on the set of CANADA'S SWEETHEART, 1985. Photo from the National Film Board of Canada.

p.24   Brittain and Sean McCann (King) on the set of THE KING CHRONICLE, 1988. Photo from the National Film Board of Canada, 3046-2AA.

p.25   Brittain, publicity still, ON GUARD FOR THEE, 1981. Photo from the National Film Board of Canada.

The Films

Title page   Brittain, publicity still, ON GUARD FOR THEE, 1981. Photo from the National Film Board of Canada.

p.29   The Canadian Memorial at Vimy Ridge. FIELDS OF SACRIFICE, 1964. Photo from the National Film Board of Canada.

p.30   Brittain, John Spotton and unidentified on location for FIELDS OF SACRIFICE, 1962. Photo from the National Film Board of Canada, S-395.

p.32   Dr. Norman Bethune in Spain, 1936. Photo from the National Film Board of Canada.

p.33   *Far left*: Bethune and General Neih Junc-Che at Wu'Tai, June 1938. Photo from the National Film Board of Canada, S-14265.

Left centre: Bethune, General Neih Junc-Che and unidentified man at Wu'Tai, June 1938. Photo from the National Film Board of Canada, S-13138.

Right centre: Bethune treating unidentified soldier, no date. Photo from the National Film Board of Canada, S-14262.

Far right: Bethune performing surgery in Buddhist Temple, 1939. Photo from the National Film Board of Canada, S-13139.

p.34   Norman Bethune in China, 1938. Photo from Canapress Photoservice.

p.36   Brittain and John Spotton at Auschwitz, MEMORANDUM, 1965. Photo from the National Film Board of Canada.

p.37   *Upper photo*: Nazi rally in Vienna, 13/3/38. Photo from Canapress Photo Service, 2462.

Lower photo: Camp survivor, 1945. Photo from Canapress Photo Service, 24926-13.

p.39   Lord Thomson of Fleet, 1976. Photo from Canapress Photo Service.

p.40   *Left*: Lord Thomson during royal ceremony. No date. Photo from Canapress Photo Service.

Right: Lord Thomson at home. No date. Photo from Canapress Photo Service.

p.41   Brittain with Lord Thomson, 1965 on location for NEVER A BACKWARD STEP. 1966.

p.43   Malcolm Lowry in England, shortly before his death, 1959. Photo from Canapress Photo Service, J6L20.

p.44. Malcolm Lowry at Dollarton Beach, British Columbia, 1953. Photo from the National Film Board of Canada, S14888.

p.46 Henry Ford, corporate photograph, circa 1915. Photo from the Western Pictorial Index.

p.47 Henry Ford II, during an interview with Donald Brittain for the film HENRY FORD'S AMERICA, 1977. Photo from the National Film Board of Canada, S-16381.

p.49. May 2, 1946, Henry Ford II, with Henry and Clara Ford in the first car Henry Ford built. Photo from Canapress Photo Service.

p.51. Fred Phipps, Canadian Broadcasting Corporation.

p.54 Aislin Cartoon, 1986. From the collection of the National Film Board of Canada.

p.55 Brittain in Rene Levesque's office, shooting THE CHAMPIONS: THE FINAL BATTLE, 1986. Photo by Rick Bujold, from the National Film Board of Canada.

p.56 Pierre Elliot Trudeau and Rene Levesque, February, 1980. Photo from Canapress Photo Service, (Ser415 PEST).

p.57 *Left*: Rene Levesque campaigning, October, 1962. Photo from Canapress Photo Service, GJF 823.

Right: Pierre Elliot Trudeau campaigning, April, 6, 1968. Photo from Canapress Photo Service, STF-CPM.

p.58. Andree Cousineau (Marie) and Maury Chaykin (Banks), on the set of CANADA'S SWEETHEART, 1985. Photo from the National Film Board of Canada, S19096.

p.59 Hal C. Banks at Norris Commission Hearings, 1962. Photo from Canapress Photo Service.

p.61 Hal C. Banks leading march on Parliament Hill, Ottawa, 1963. Photo from Canapress Photo Service.

p.62 Brittain with Sean McCann (King) on the set of THE KING CHRONICLE, 1988. Photo from the National Film Board of Canada, 3080-4A.

p.64 William Lyon Mackenzie King, Franklin Roosevelt and Winston Churchill at the Quebec Conference, 1943. Photo from Canapress Photo Service. (CPT 4-8-8).

p.65. William Lyon Mackenzie King and Pat #1 at Kingsmere. Photo by Karsh, from the collection of the National Film Board of Canada, ON GUARD FOR THEE, S-17906.

p.66 William Lyon Mackenzie King at Kingsmere, no date. Photo from Canapress Photo Service.

Film Awards

Title Page   Brittain with Genie. Photo from Canapress Photo Service, 1986.

Filmography

Title Page   Photo from the National Film Board of Canada, FIELDS OF SACRIFICE, S-399.

Honours and Distinctions

Title Page   Academy of Canadian Cinema and Television, 1986.

Biography

Title page   Brittain on the set of the KING CHRONICLE. Fred Phipps, Canadian Broadcasting Corporation, 1988

Bibliography

Title page   Brittain in the NFB Reference Library, National Film Board of Canada.

Credits

Title page   Brittain on location for VOLCANO.

Back Cover:

Brittain on the set of CANADA'S SWEETHEART with Andreas Poulsson, Susan Trow, Claudette Messier and unidentified, 1985. Photo from the National Film Board of Canada.